Plan A

The Transformation of Argentina's Economy

GUNTER PAULI

(author of The Blue Economy)

with JURRIAAN KAMP

(editor)

JJK Books (English Edition)
2020 Alameda Padre Serra, Suite 135 Santa Barbara CA 93103
Phone: (415) 595-6451
www.jjkbooks.com

Ordering Information
Quantity sales. Special discounts are available on quantity purchases by corporations, associations, and others. For details, contact JJK Books at the address above. Orders for college textbook/course adoption use. Please contact JJK Books at the address above.

Library of Congress Cataloging-in-Publication Data
ISBN: 978-0-692-18765-4

Cover and interior design: Rick Greer
Copy Editor:
Production service: Rick Greer

Plan A

The Transformation of Argentina's Economy

GUNTER PAULI
(author of The Blue Economy)

with JURRIAAN KAMP
(editor)

JJK Books

The way to solutions

Argentinian Map of Opportunities

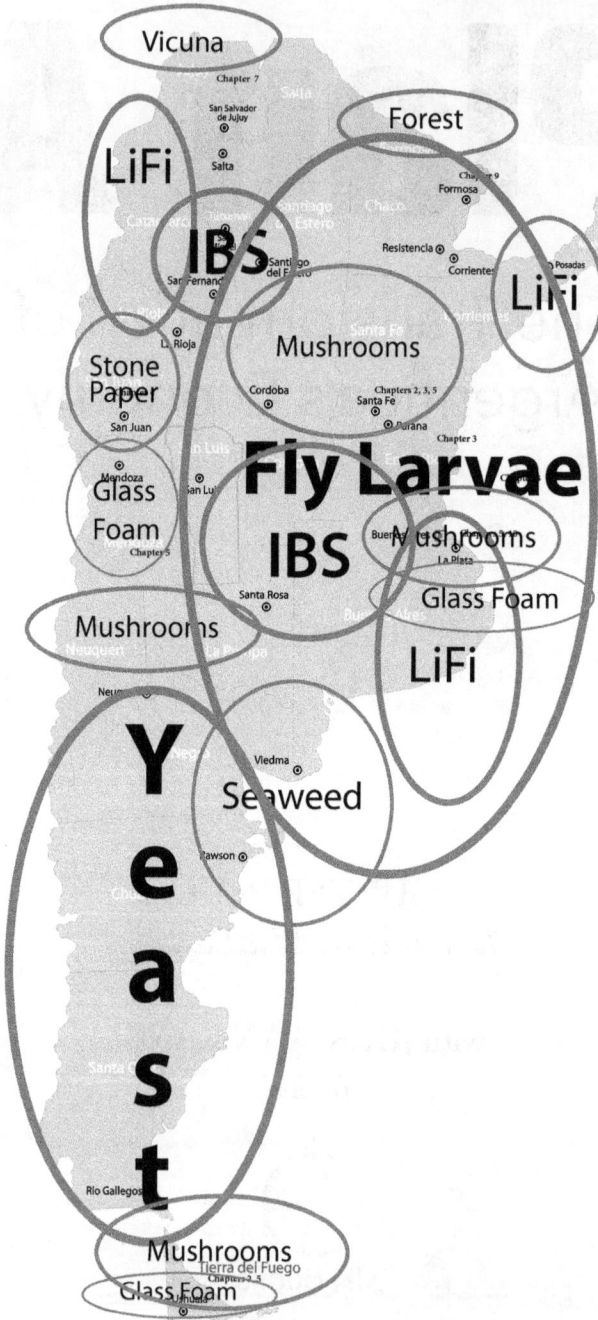

Contents

Plan A

Executive Summary

Argentina has the great potential to launch at least ten new economic activities to transform its economy. Each one of these opportunities is based on available resources. These include raw materials that are locally accessible in abundance and an existing infrastructure for transportation and processing. Science confirms the proposed opportunities for groundbreaking economic transformation.

This transformation is possible—the know-how is sufficiently widespread, and where the skills may be lacking, the desire to learn and act has been noted. The international investor community is alert. When the right policy framework accompanies these proposals, the passage from concept to implementation can be swiftly pursued.

Some of these innovative business models may surprise policymakers, entrepreneurs, and investors, however, each one has been tested as relevant in the particular circumstances. The first objective of this portfolio of activities is to offer policymakers and investors options to outperform what is on offer today. Argentina has the opportunity to transform its economy based on commodities and big-scale industrial processes to an economy based on value-added products capable of responding to the basic needs of all. This transformation will also ensure Argentina is in a competitive position because it is built on the country's unique assets.

This outline—Plan A—is but the first, but it sets a clear mark to rebuild Argentina's brand with initiatives inspiring the social activist, the environmental pioneer, the new-found entrepreneur, and the impact investor.

Acknowledgements and a Word about the Methodology

T his book is the distillate of a year of work.

We involved hundreds of people, undertook dozens of trips, visited the four corners of Argentina, shared our insights with thousands, and addressed diverse audiences from students, and the unemployed to farmers, chambers of commerce, indigenous communities, artists, industrialists, journalists, academia, and the government.

The Cabinet of the Minister of Environment and Sustainable Development's extraordinary team led by Minister Rabino Sergio Bergman has been instrumental in ensuring this process was efficient and far-reaching.

The support from the Club of Rome's Argentinian and an inspiring circle of leaders and change-makers—Daniel Van Lierde, Gustavo Grobocopatel, Darío Werthein, Javier Gronda, Elisa Parodi, Mauro Toscani, Alberto Hensel, Raúl Tello, Omar Perotti, Luis Castellano, María Inés Zigaran, and Kris Tompkins—have been a tremendous support. I am indebted to them.

The identification of the opportunities we present in this book underwent a rigorous process. First, we defined the underpinning science. Once the international scientific community provided unequivocal support, we solicited a signal of interest from the entrepreneurial community and world of investors. Armed with feedback from these three sectors, we modeled the impact of the proposal on the region.

This process was coordinated by a team that has been guided for years by Charles van der Haegen and Yusuke Saraya from the ZERI coordination centers in Brussels and Tokyo.

There is the need to undertake first-hand tests from the business innovators themselves. Several came in person to Argentina to offer us resounding confirmation that these opportunities were stable and ready for execution. The visits of Henry Liang (stone paper) and Joost Wouters (seaweed to gas) offered what was needed: a hands-on confirmation that this was real.

The Blue Economy works with available resources and searches to have an impact on the territory. We need to map this impact on the resilience of the community, the generation of jobs and the strengthening of resilience while responding to their basic needs on the environment, putting nature back on its evolutionary and symbiotic path, and on the business, which needs to compete solidly and effectively by generating value. This is framed and mastered through a mathematical modeling process known as "system dynamics."

This exercise was coordinated by François Nolet, a graduate in business from ICHEC Business School in Brussels, Belgium who took the opportunity to share his modeling skills as a crash course in designing development. He learned a lot in the process and succeeded in teaching all of us how vast the implications are.

Subsequently, we need to submit the effort to an acid test: will investors agree these are the opportunities to create a legacy? Mariana Bozesan and Tom Schulz, proprietors of AQAL Capital, facilitated with the European Business Angels Network (EBAN), a platform permitting us to test the ground before some 200 family offices. The results were more than encouraging. They deserve our gratitude for putting Argentina and these innovative business models on the map.

A special word of thanks to Professor Lucio Brusch de Fraga and Professor Carlos Bernal Quintero, the founder and president of ZERI Brasil Foundation and ZERI Latin America (based in Bogota) for their personal involvement alongside everyone else who ensured the high ethical and methodological standards accompany the hard work style and content that I am sure will surprise many.

Finally, we translated all core concepts into fables. Our proposals are often dismissed as fantasy, however, we forget that our present production and consumption model lives in a world of fantasy, that we consume more than the carrying capacity of our ecosystems. This is why we present the innovations in layman's terms to inspire everyone to consider this "fantasy" as a reality.

Plan A

This book would not have been possible without the personal commitment of editor Jurriaan Kamp. He lost a few sleepless nights over this project but finished it in time in spite of the tight deadlines.

With deep gratitude to all,

The ZERI Team

Foreword

In 1991, when I wrote the first article on the need to embrace the concept of zero waste and zero-emissions, little did I realize that everyone would criticize me for being unscientific (did I not know of the second law of thermodynamics?) and unrealistic (did I not understand it would cost too much and therefore make the business uncompetitive?).

Only a year later, I welcomed 500 guests to the inauguration of the first zero-emissions factory, a wooden structure with its own wastewater treatment that captured its organic volatiles on its grass roof, and where everything solid was recycled. I bought my workers Patagonia underwear, knowing the high cost would be largely compensated by the reduced cost of energy on the shop floor. There were only seven parking places in front of the building, since I paid staff to cycle to work—building parking is expensive; riding to work is healthy. It is great for the planet, as well. I knew we could do it if we put our minds to it. We might even enjoy it, save money, and get healthy while reaping great returns.

Japanese management principles inspired me: zero accidents should be the goal on the shop floor, and total quality equaled zero defects. Might the concept of zero-emissions and zero waste be the logical extension? Though I saw this clearly, apparently, no one else did. As a global citizen on a mission to change the world for the better, I concluded there was no point in further debate—the only way to convince them was to expose those who were and are prepared to see what we have done. While the projects were small—my factory did not even have 100 employees—the joy was great when supermarkets were pressed to put my detergents on the shelves, when we harvested the first mushrooms on coffee grounds, and we fed the first spent substrate to a chicken. The first initiatives in Fiji, Colombia, and Namibia soon expanded and diversified, and before I knew it, the natural dynamics of the good created a portfolio of the most diverse ideas with the most diverse partners resulting in the most diverse initiatives with tangible results.

As time and all of these initiatives evolved, I realized I was had not just realized a dream—I had gone beyond my dreams. I had not only inspired people to dream again—I was empowering them to stop being negative and against. I empowered them to join the drive to change the rules of the game, create a new, competitive industry, to respond to people's needs, and strengthen the commons. This would give a sense of maturity in life and an energy that characterized everyone in our broad network of scientists, scholars, entrepreneurs, and educators.

As we started designing projects transforming tiny, first steps into transformations like Gaviotas (regenerating a forest) and El Hierro (re-launching the economy of a depopulated island), we saw that the demand was great and the pull was strong. Would I see opportunities beyond coffee and tea and islands and the sea? Travels to more than 150 countries and a relentless rhythm of discovery and envisioning and embracing new realities left me with a sense of enthusiasm that tended to be contagious. I am incapable of overlooking the good, even in the wake of the worst, such as a dilapidated gold mine in Ghana, a desertification in Mongolia, or a decommissioned petrochemical plant with asbestos in Italy.

The first projects had an impact on a few families (Tsumeb Brewery in Namibia), a school (Montfort Boys Town in Fiji), a community (Las Gaviotas in Colombia), an island (El Hierro in Spain), a province (Limburg in Belgium), an agricultural zone (Eje Cafetero in Colombia), a coffee company (Lavazza), a pasta maker (Barilla), a region (Brittany in France), and an industry (biopolymers in Italy and gold mining in Ghana and Colombia), but then the scope extended to mega cities (Johannesburg in South Africa), nations (Argentina) and sub-continents (11 island states in the South Pacific).

Demand for our creative input with respect to transforming unknown assets into new portfolios of industry is rapidly on the rise, and the only limiting factor is our creative capacity to respond. There is a clear willingness to design new business models and economic growth scenarios that go beyond the proposals and build on the desire to move from idea to reality, from concept to implementation. This report is the distillation of the first and most relevant findings in Argentina, a project at the request of the highest authorities of the nation. It is not our job to define new strategies for Argentina—we wish to contribute to the objective the government has stated: the transformation to a more competitive nation better able to respond to the basic needs of all, including the millions of living creatures that are a part of the ecosystem.

For the first time, the size, scope, speed, and scale policymakers, investors, business leaders, and pioneers from NGOs are ready to embrace permits us to see the impact on statistics this window of opportunity can have. There is no doubt that we need to start having an impact, but that willingness has never been so great. It is important that we clarify the team from ZERI and the Blue Economy are not the wonder boys and girls that make magic happen. We have sensed and finally articulated the trends permitting us to surf the waves and create a difference, first of all, because we subject every out-of-the-box idea to the scientists and ensure there is a minimum of truth in each statement. We only observe what there is and imagine—on the basis of science—what there could be. Once this has been ascertained, whatever we propose makes business and societal sense for the Captains of Legacy. Armed with this, we are ready to change the world one step at the time, but run faster and longer than ever before, because we know we can do better.

What an honor to have been asked by the President of Argentina to reflect on the future of this great nation that I first visited in 1976. I have always been convinced that it has a greater future than realized to date. After one year of intensive work with my 150 colleagues who have guided and inspired, there is the sense that this nation can shift from scarcity to abundance, from unemployment to full employment, from chemistry and genetics to putting its grand ecosystems and Nature back on its evolutionary path. There is no doubt in my mind that Argentina can turn into a competitive force with an economic model based on what it has, generating value and satisfying the needs of all. What a privilege to join this endeavor. I started this mission with passion, and I will continue it with pride.

Gunter Pauli

Plan A

An opportunity for 'Captains of Legacy'

This book is about the transformation of Argentina's economy. The dictionary reads: "transformation: A seemingly miraculous change in form." Argentina seeks fundamental change. It wants to build an economy serving the needs of its people. These needs include a healthy and sustainable environment and the urgent generation of jobs to reverse the impoverishment that has characterized more than a decade of crises. It is not Argentina's objective to catch up on industrial policies that have produced widespread pollution and waste in other countries—Argentina doesn't want more of the same. The present political and business leadership looks for innovations and breakthroughs achieving bold goals. It wants to lead and to inspire its citizens and the wider world. It wants a miracle, indeed. As we shall see, such a miracle can be achieved. In fact, Argentina cannot fail if the country is prepared to embrace creative insights offered by science and experience and follow the laws that have been creating abundance in nature since the beginnings of time.

Plan A

In the late 1800s, Argentina was a "go to" place. The country showed great progress and—from a European perspective—more potential than Brazil, Mexico, and even the United States. Buenos Aires developed as the Paris of Latin America with wide avenues and gorgeous buildings. Argentina's soil seemed richer and more productive than anywhere else, fed by an abundance of water. Its wealthy future as a rich nation seemed secure. Many ventured across the Atlantic Ocean to come to this land of bonanza, work for a decade or two, and return home rich.

Some 125 years later, after decades of political and economic upheaval, Argentina has lost its historic excellence but still possesses vast natural wealth and resources. It is the eighth-largest country in the world, spread out over almost three million square kilometers and with access to 3.3 million square kilometers of territorial seas, doubling the economic potential for the nation, as we will see throughout this book. The country is divided into 18 eco-regions, with incredible biological diversity and fertility. Under a new government, Argentina seeks an opportunity to shine, once again. The country has the potential, but it needs the boldness and clarity of vision to act.

The Government of President Mauricio Macri (2016-2020) realizes that a transformation of the economy requires more than fresh investments to "update" existing industries. It requires more than a reset or a catch-up. The World Bank states that Argentina is "currently undergoing an economic transformation that promotes sustainable economic development with social inclusion and integration in the global economy," yet Argentina is still listed as a "developing nation." This term implies a country halfway on a journey to earning it the status of "developed" when it reaches some undefined finish line.

It is a misleading and misguided trajectory, easily illustrated with two figures. Today, the average Argentinean produces 341 kilograms of waste per year, whereas the average American produces 733 kilograms. Surely, Argentina's goal can't be to follow the American journey of "progress" only to increase the production of waste in its society. True wealth requires more than the wasteful, polluting, economic "development" as we know it. In fact, as we shall see in this book, true wealth can be acquired without disproportionate financial investments by simply using, and thus cleaning up, waste and idle resources, by adding value to things that have no value today. Quality of life cannot solely be created by restrictive policies constraining industry as it pursues its goals. There is the need to expose established industries, as well as entrepreneurs, to a portfolio of opportunities that outperform the present. This is the main goal of this report, called Plan A, where the "A" stands for Argentina. We do not believe there is a Plan B: Argentina has to focus on what it can achieve with the available resources.

The resilient and productive economies of the future will succeed in following nature's inspiration. The challenge of modern society is that most of our economy—from farming to industry, from banking to the Internet— ignores nature or even works against nature. Our societies and systems— deliberately, in many ways—defy basic laws underpinning the functioning of our world. We do not grasp incredible chances to respond to people's needs for water, food, health, housing, energy, and jobs, converting readily available resources into products and services produced and consumed within carrying capacity.

Our level of ignorance is sometimes surprising. We spend massive amounts of energy to overcome gravity—from elevators to water-distribution systems and air-conditioning—yet we never bother to watch an apple grow. This is not a romantic reflection—this is a scientific observation. Why are we taught how the apple comes down from the tree according to the law of gravity? Why has no one bothered explaining an alternate series of seven laws of physics allowing the apple to defy the law of gravity prior to subjecting itself to it? As long as we only look at the law of gravity, how can we imagine more energy-efficient techniques?

Plan A proposes to explain how "Argentinian apples" get up in the tree and serve society while achieving levels of efficiency considered "impossible to reach" by many. If one only uses today's technologies and business models, the proposals in this book have no chance at all. If, however, we are prepared to go beyond reason, to innovate with positive disruptions, the economy will be rapidly transformed. Plan A sets the stage for surprising competitive proposals to unsettle the present understanding. Science and concrete cases substantiate each proposition, around the world. We know the only response to incredulity is to suggest a visit to where these businesses have been implemented to witness the new realities that have been created. The brief descriptions in this book are backed up by science and research in detailed reports, available at request.

Following natural principles means to leave centuries of linear thinking behind to embrace a systems-approach to evolution and change. It poses a challenge for us to see and accept the potential for transformation in non-linear ways, cascading matter, nutrition, and energy like cycles in ecosystems. You cannot "plan" a rainforest, but once you get a rainforest going, change is deeper, more fundamental and more rewarding than anything that could have been achieved with old-fashioned planning (see chapter 9).

Nature has overcome nearly every imaginable challenge over the past millions of years. We should follow the time-tested design principles nature uses to produce food, cycle water, regenerate soil, and ensure all members of the ecosystem succeed on their evolutionary and symbiotic paths. Nature has an incredibly efficient business model: there's no waste in nature, no pollution, and no unemployment. Nature is never concerned about its "core business" or "economies of scale." Nature respects limits. A tree "knows" that if it gets to 100 feet tall, there's no point in going to 500 feet. In nature, there's collaboration—a symbiosis—to respond to everyone's needs in the system. In nature, we can discover how to turn that 90-plus percent waste our economies generate into new value, transforming scarcity into abundance, unemployment into jobs, and hunger into healthy diets. In the process, we can, in fact, restore much of the damage done, putting nature back on its evolutionary path, generating tens of thousands of jobs and rebuilding communities.

A systems-approach means that we look across the boundaries of existing industries to discover new benefits.

Plan A

When we cultivate seaweed to produce biogas, we not only replace fossil fuels, we also produce fertilizer and animal feed, and we regenerate marine environments, helping re-establish fish stocks. When we introduce the manufacture of stone paper as a model for cleaning the mining industry's waste, we also battle deforestation, soil depletion, and climate change. The ten business models for Argentina in this book each provide multiple benefits for society, entrepreneurs, and investors. Multiple benefits mean multiple cash flows, which means more flexibility, less risk, and more resilience, just as in nature.

In these examples and models, a government cannot lead with a traditional "department structure." Ministers have to work together across departmental lines because "seaweed" belongs to the Department of Energy as much as to the Department of Fisheries and Health and Agriculture. This requires as much innovation and dedication at the state level as it requires clarity amongst entrepreneurs and investors that the common denominator is a redefinition of competitiveness. All stakeholders need to jointly discover how and where Argentina benefits most in terms of value generated in the economy.

The models in this book require minimal investment and provide short or mid-term payback. A mushroom farm (chapter 2) can be started with 500 dollars with the money recouped in two weeks. A seaweed farm can be started with 25,000 dollars per hectare with the investment coming back in three years while accumulating sufficient cash flow to self-finance growth which can evolve into a multi-billion dollar initiative. A small fly larvae factory can be started with 50,000 dollars, which can be earned back in one year. A foam glass plant needs an investment of two million dollars, which can be recouped in five years. The manufacturing of stone paper requires the biggest investment, with more than 100 million dollars per mill, but even that investment can be earned back in some three to five years. Each of these projects—from the small to the large—offer returns in excess of 20 percent.

Yes, all of these models provide swift and healthy returns, but this is about more than money. Remember: this is about the transformation of the Argentinean economy and society. It is about regenerating damaged ecosystems and (re)building healthy communities. It is about showing the world how a truly vibrant society develops. It is about launching a wave of creativity and entrepreneurship that radiates confidence in the future for new generations.

This is why we need a force to harness this creative energy. The message of history is clear: there is no more powerful force to drive innovation and change than human enterprise. Decades of well-funded, non-profit initiatives dedicated to solving humanity's most pressing problems—from malaria to malnutrition—have alleviated the worst of them, but have not changed the world. And, yes, governments can have a big impact and facilitate and support outcomes for the common good through regulation and tax policies, however, as we have witnessed with the action required to reverse climate change, policymakers are not capable of taking the bold decisions required to turn statistics around.

In the end, only enterprising pioneers and their "angel"

investors can lead fundamental innovation and transformation. Without the entrepreneurial drive and the capital to support it, we will only witness more of the same. Plan A is not just a plan for transformation—it is also an investment strategy and with good reason: no initiative can sustain social and environmental goals over time unless it assured the continuous flow of revenue and building up of capital. If critical social and environmental initiatives depend on subsidies or charity, they are at risk and will likely face disruptions.

We do, however, face a challenge. As we have seen, business, as we know it today, has become a force that serves a few at the expense of many as well as the environment on which all life depends. The highest entrepreneurial achievements today are initiatives like Facebook and Uber that create billion for a few people from services unable to respond to the most basic needs of people around the world. In the past, steel and railway barons also became extremely wealthy, but their contributions were arguably more related to common interests and needs.

We have even invented a new category of business to describe activities supporting society at large. We talk about "responsible business" and "social entrepreneurs." These are great initiatives, but like the nonprofits, they haven't had a major impact on changing business' overall negative and destructive course in today's world. The terms "responsible business" and "social entrepreneurs" sound like "organic apples." In the strange in which we live, it has become normal to treat natural fruit, like apples, with an assortment of artificial, unhealthy substances to "protect" it against insects, et cetera. As a result, there are people growing natural apples, called "organic apples." We have given a new name to something that was always there: an apple that falls from a tree is…well, an apple. Shouldn't we have, instead, given the new, treated apple its own name, like a chemical apple?

Similarly, there is only one objective for business: to provide products and services to serve the interests of society while creating value. This is why corporations receive licenses to operate. Instead of calling businesses serving the common good "responsible" or "social," we should call the degenerated version of modern businesses "irresponsible" or "destructive." There is power in words; they help us understand what we are doing.

It is not that long ago that business and society were on parallel paths. In fact, the world has radically changed in a mere two generations, as the following anecdote illustrates.

Some twenty years ago, the son of Frits Philips—the then almost 100-year- old former CEO of the multinational electronics company of the same name and son of its founder, Anton Philips—was watching the evening news with his father. The news was about Philips closing factories in Asia and laying off employees. The report concluded that the share price of the company had risen after the announcements. Father Philips reacted shocked that the managing director of the Philips factory had spoken about its closure without so much as a word about the pain and sadness of the people who were going to lose their jobs.

Philips Senior continued, lecturing his son: "Why do you think we opened a factory in Drachten (a town in the poorer northern part of the Netherlands, far away from the Philips headquarters in the south of the country) after World War II? Of course, that was inconvenient for us, but that was where people needed work."

In other words, only a few decades prior, Philips knew it carried an economic and social responsibility in and for society. Some ten years before, Ratan Tata, then chairman of India's largest industrial conglomerate, the Tata Group—one that is almost completely owned by philanthropic trusts— said after the acquisition of the British-Dutch steel company, Corus: "We earn money to give it away. I want to go to bed every night knowing that I haven't hurt anyone." These are very rare words to be spoken by an entrepreneur these days.

We may have to wait a long time before the mainstream world of government and business redesigns the rules of the business game so the corporate world will serve society again. It also clear that business as usual will not solve humanity's problems. We have work to do. There are massive opportunities for transformation in the interest of billions of people. Rather than depending on "captains of industry" who nowadays only seem to pray to the gods of greed and money, we need nourish the emergence of the *Captains of Legacy* (please note: these captains, entrepreneurs, and investors, are women and men but we will—respectfully to both sexes— write about them in the masculine sense). You hardly create a meaningful legacy when you develop a computer program and make a few billions to give away to good causes. Captains of Legacy don't make money in the old way to give it back the right way. Captains of Legacy give their best creative energy to transforming the world into a better society, working in harmony with nature, dedicated to doing better all the time. While doing so, they make their money over time. Their children and grandchildren may even make a lot of money, and there is nothing wrong with that, however, their priority is always meeting the needs of society: alleviating poverty, generating jobs, and restoring nature.

Let's be careful with the word, "legacy." The legacy doesn't have to be a great invention (a battery that can be made without non-renewable metals) or a big industry. A legacy can be an idea, an approach that leads to transformation— such as mushroom farming—that can be copied by millions around the globe. A new generation of millennials is making clear, on a daily basis, that they stand ready to contribute, and differently than their parents. They are natural members of the new tribe of Captains of Legacy. To get them going—as well as anyone who wants to contribute to putting communities and nature back on their evolutionary paths—we first need to identify portfolios of opportunities with locally available resources.

Yvon Chouinard of the outdoor gear manufacturer, Patagonia, arguably one of the most successful, sustainable enterprises, never went to college. He started his company to provide climbing gear for his friends so that he would have money to go rock climbing, as well. Chouinard responded to a need. The fundamental flaw is this: we cannot subject and limit entrepreneurship to managerial techniques that created the industries dominating today. Entrepreneurship is in the first place to identify and respond to needs, which requires an ability to get out of the box and navigate unchartered environments—it does not require a market study to define needs. You only need to open your eyes to determine whether there is the need for jobs, clean water, or healthy food, and to conclude that what has been done so far has not changed the needs. This is the purpose of our scan of Argentina and our search for identifying chances others have not yet seen.

Once a Captain of Legacy has identified needs, his next assignment is to look beyond the obvious. This is why he doesn't need a clever book by an expert on how to generate clean drinking water in ten simple steps—if there were an obvious solution, it would have been implemented by now. The mission is to take a fresh look at what is locally available. An entrepreneur needs to create value in response to needs while using what is readily available. He imagines solutions embodied in products and services that no one has visualized before. Apple's Steve Jobs was a master of this process of designing something everyone wanted, and nobody realized they were missing.

For the Captain of Legacy, an abundance of readily available resources, including labor, in the local environment is a critical starting point. This is how we approached the task entrusted to us by the Argentinean government. We can always spot the necessary abundance. Abundance of resources allows for a competitive proposition and a disruptive approach to the market, which is what we need, because we want to fast-track innovation to respond to the pressing challenges of poverty, hunger, or loss of species that cannot afford patience or an investment "burn rate" where a lot of money is spent before any tangible results are achieved. All Plan A proposals have a break-even point calculated as a net-accumulated cash flow of less than years.

While the entrepreneur should not exercise patience in response to basic needs, he should avoid rushing to producing or designing one product or service right away. Rather, the challenge is to oversee the system of which any product or service is a part. It is impossible to know and understand the complexity of the system from the start. For the same reason—counter to traditional, old-fashioned business models taught at MBA schools—the goal is not to have one product sold to one customer. Rather, the objective is to have an interactive platform of customers creating an integrated portfolio of products and services that will ultimately transform society.

This also means it is of great importance to continuously discover and explore. Plan A contains an initial review of the ten most relevant initiatives. Its aim is to create and inspire a culture of innovation. Nature keeps evolving, responding, and filling new niches. The hardest thing for an entrepreneur—indeed, for any human being—is to always keep a beginner's mind. The current project may very well be only a small stepping stone to the next, bigger step with more impact than you can imagine today, but you can only find that next, biggest opportunity when you are not fixated on what you have at hand. Over time, when understanding of natural processes grows, the system-platform approach to enterprise will become second nature. The platform—or the community— also reduces risks, which is another important condition for the resilience and ongoing success of the enterprise.

When the need is clear and great, and the abundant local resources have been identified, the Captain of Legacy can launch a portfolio of solutions—his business model—quickly and without the need for substantial (financial) investments, so long as he knows his first customers. Each of the proposals points toward the abundant resources and clients in waiting. The farming of mushrooms provides a good example (see chapter 2). Imagine a group of orphans that starts farming mushrooms to sell to local restaurants and stores. This will be a high-risk venture that won't easily attract interest or investment. The orphans have no business experience—why would any restaurant buy their mushrooms? If, on the other hand, the orphans begin by collecting spent coffee grounds from the restaurants, they will find support and collaboration, because they solve a problem: they collect waste. If they subsequently turn that waste into mushrooms, the restaurants will be interested, because the orphans have added value to "their" waste. In other words: the first paying customers can easily and clearly be identified, and that gets the business going.

In the current business paradigm of perceived scarcity, protection is key. Innovations are hidden in patents. At best, a new, successful concept is distributed through a franchise model. There are some 37,000 McDonalds outlets in the world, serving 68 million people every day. It took 70 years to build the company into what it is today. This may seem impressive, however, 800+ million people suffer from malnutrition worldwide. The McDonalds model—irrespective of the quality of the fast food—is clearly not going to solve that problem anytime soon. This is why innovative business models, open-source principles, and sharing insights as to how to succeed is vital.

Mushroom farming works everywhere, although the opportunities will be different according to local circumstances. When the experiences are freely shared, the opportunity can spread fast. Chido Govera began farming mushrooms in 1997. Twenty years later, some 5,000 mushrooms projects are rebuilding local communities around the world. If we take that to one million, it's enough for a lot of people to earn a good living. To get there, there is no need for a boardroom, a market analysis, or investment plan that gravely slows growth, development, constrains action, and blocks creativity. With transparency, mushroom farming can, indeed, feed hundreds of millions of people and make a serious contribution to the malnutrition challenge. Remember: our true reality is abundance. There is no limited cake forcing people to fight for the largest piece, but an ever-growing cake of new opportunities that keeps adding multiple benefits for more and more people. This is what the Captain of Legacy wants to achieve; this is what we envision for Argentina.

The opportunities are endless. Mushroom farmers will discover that not only does their customer-restaurant have spent coffee grounds after serving their clients—they also serve them fresh orange juice, and at the end of the day, they have a container full of orange peels—why shouldn't the farmer collect those as well? One kilogram of citrus peels, one liter of water, and seven spoons of sugar in a glass container will be enough to produce, within a few weeks and without any need for energy, one liter of fresh, orange-smelling soap that can be used as dishwashing liquid, hand soap, shampoo, or floor cleaner. Some transformations can even turn it into an effective toilet and bathroom cleaner. Do you think the restaurant would be interested in sharing this local soap with its clients in its bathrooms?

As we will see in chapter 2, there's much more you can do with coffee grounds. When you build an integrated, open source platform of producers and consumers, there will be a continuous weaving of opportunities, leading to a key characteristic of the Captain of Legacy: he has self-imposed an ongoing responsibility to generate value. When the next, bigger opportunity arises, he has to act and accept the challenge.

Our world does not make enough progress in responding to urgent, basic needs as great projects and opportunities are not pursued because we are ignorant of them. Our greatest obstacle in economic growth is the fact that we copy what the world does and ignore what the new world might invent. It is a moral duty to ensure that more value is created so that more needs can be served by building on relevant, pioneering cases. This is an important task of Plan A. Given the tasks, the challenges can reach beyond generations. It took 40 years to restore the rainforest in Las Gaviotas to the level it has achieved today. It may take even longer to replant mangroves to protect coastal zones and establish seaweed plantations around the world, but is time a problem? Many travelers are inspired when they visit the medieval cathedrals spread across Europe. Most of these cathedrals were built over the course of more than a century. This means that visionary leaders determined to endow their city with a cathedral would never see the final work of art and architecture, and they knew it. The carpenters and sculptors knew they were not going to enjoy the finished results of their work in their lifetimes. Still, everyone believed in the project and was inspired and motivated to contribute money and talent for generations to come. This is the role and responsibility of the Captain of Legacy. This is also what we imagine for Argentina with this simple and short Plan A.

After decades of destruction, the rebuilding of communities and the restoration of nature will be like building cathedrals. We need captains of legacy, entrepreneurs, and investors, who, like the cathedral carpenters, believe that you can change the course of—and transform—society and the planet. This book shows that many cathedrals are waiting to be built in Argentina and around the world, while some are already under construction. This is an invitation for Captains of Legacy in Argentina and beyond to join this rewarding and inspiring journey of transformation.

Fable 1

Masters and grandmasters

The Captains of Legacy invest time and money in endeavors that will change the direction of a community. This requires a unique learning environment. Since innovations are not known, and the new business models have yet to turn mainstream, the pedagogy required to create this fundamental shift implies that the masters will learn from their students. This is a precious lesson from Asia.

Two students are worrying about their exams. Their tough professor has proposed that those who can ask him a question in their subject field that he cannot properly answer will get full marks on the exam.

"I think this is a trick," says one student.

"No, it's not! It's a way to challenge us to learn better and more," replies another student.

"But why?"

"Because if we want to ask him a question he has no clue about, we must first know everything he knows."

"That means to get full marks, we must be as smart as he is. Forget it! We'd better learn everything he's taught us by heart."

"How boring it must be for him to sit there and listen to students telling him everything he already knows over and over again."

"Exactly. How refreshing will it be for him to learn something about his specialty that he has never heard before?"

"If we ask him a question he cannot answer, it will make him think."

"Any professor will be upset if you trouble his mind."

"This professor is different, I guarantee you. This is why he is considered a master, a true sensei."

"Imagine you are a master and every year you have hundreds of new students coming to show you that they have learned something from you. Better for them to show that they have been inspired."

"Then the master will be inspired."

"Imagine that, each year, there are a few students who bring him new ideas, new theories, and new cases. What happens to the master? He will learn from his students by teaching the best he knows!"

"They say that the best masters have students who are better than the master ever was."

"That is the only way there will be innovation, progress, and creativity. There is so much needed to make a better world."

"Imagine if all we do is to learn what our parents and teachers know and nothing more. There would be no progress."

"Yes, but since the master has many students, he learns a lot, while the students will only learn from the master."

"This is how our professor can become the Grand Master."

"And this is how students become new masters."

"If the Grand Master learns from the best students who turn into masters—some of which, one day, may also be Grand Masters—and he shares everything he knows and learns, then he could even become immortal and be remembered forever."

... And it only has just begun!

Argentinian Map of Opportunities

PART A
The Protein Strategy

Plan A

Chapter 1

Doubling protein production with fly larvae

A rgentina produces protein for 400 million people. That's a remarkable achievement for a nation of 44 million people. Even more remarkable is that Argentina could do substantially better while improving marine and land environments. Using fly larvae, Argentina can convert the waste of the meat production into fresh protein that can be fed to poultry and fish. By only using waste, Argentina can increase its protein output by more than 30 percent. This new activity will generate new economic development, income, and jobs. In the process, Argentina would clean up its environment and reduce deforestation and the pressure on scarce water resources while supporting the regeneration of fish stock, yet another source of protein. Contrary to common understanding, the generation of more protein could actually clean up the environment. This innovative approach, tested at scale, has attracted major investments and is in the process of a global rollout. Argentina has the ability to join and possibly even lead this bandwagon.

The current, global meat consumption is about 320 million

tons per year. Include the 93 million tons from the fishing industry and 74 million tons from fish cultivation, and the total animal protein consumption reaches almost 500 million tons. While meat consumption in Western countries is decreasing through the adoption of healthier diets, rising standards of living in the rest of the world result in people eating greater quantities of meat. Global animal protein consumption is expected to rise to 700 million tons by 2050. Today, there are 19 billion chickens, 1.5 billion cows, one billion pigs, and one billion sheep living on the planet, and a trillion fingerlings on fish farms—all of these animals need to be fed.

These numbers indicate the enormous demand for animal feed. Globally, 98 percent of soybeans, 34 percent of all grain production, and 33 percent of the fish catch is used to feed animals. The race to feed is, in the end, a race to produce more protein. High-quality protein is converted into a higher quality at a high conversion cost. Increasing grain and soybean production depletes soil and water resources and increases deforestation. Feeding fish with fish generates pressure on marine environments. As a result, 75 percent of the world's fish stocks are in dangerous decline.

There is simply no way to keep feeding more and more animals beyond the carrying capacity of the earth without seriously damaging natural environments—a radical innovation is required. In order to secure a solid response to demand, one needs to think outside the box and beyond the beaten track to pave the way for innovation and the creation of new industries. High-tech solutions include the cultivation of meat cells in reactors in the absence of animals. IndieBio is a biotech accelerator that backs startups aiming to redefine food production, reduce the environmental impact, and end cruelty to animals. "The aim is to ensure that people keep eating what they love, but to produce it in a way, so it's not damaging the planet," says IndieBio's co-founder, Ryan Bethencourt, who is vegan.

Memphis Meats is an IndieBio success. The company generated headlines last year with the creation of the world's first lab-grown meatball. The company has subsequently succeeded in making "clean" chicken and duck (without the need to raise and kill the animals for their meat). Its CEO, Uma Valeti, says the process involves taking tiny meat cells from an animal (via a painless biopsy or sample), which are fed nutrients enabling the cells to grow until they eventually turn into edible meat. The environmental impact of reducing the world's cattle herds, which are major emitters of methane, would be profound. "If the US switched to Memphis Meats beef, we would expect the greenhouse gas reduction to be like taking almost 23m cars off the road. One burger could save the amount of water used in 51 showers," Valeti says. A recent survey suggests that 65 percent of people would give "in-vitro" or "cultured meat" a try.

A country like Argentina that has such a vast extension of land does not have a competitive position in this hi-tech, hi-capital game. Its territories and resources are ideal for innovations embracing lo-tech and low-capital. This is the solution of producing protein through cultivating insects. Most people cringe at the thought of eating insects despite the fact that over 1,000 species of insects are eaten in 80 percent of the world's nations. Animals, however, such as chicken, trout, and salmon, are used to eating insects. In fact, fishermen use insects as bait to catch fish, and no one has minded that.

Studies show that fly larvae have a high nutritional value and are a reliable source of food. Fly larvae can have protein levels of 60 percent compared to 35 percent for soybean flour. This means there is an enormous opportunity to relieve the pressure on growing protein for animal feed by shifting to the cultivation of insects. The best part of this solution is that waste is the only thing we need to cultivate insects. Argentina—which processes both animals in slaughterhouses and grains in mills—is, therefore, strategically and ideally positioned to embark on this highly productive process with solid returns and convincing environmental credentials.

In other words, we can grow much more protein with a free resource Argentina already has in abundance. The immediate focus would be on the waste of slaughterhouses, and the leftovers of restaurants and supermarkets that often seriously pollute water systems and overburden landfills today. The combination of both industrial-scale waste streams in a rural environment and the reduction of food waste in an urban environment offers investment opportunities that benefit from a guaranteed supply (the waste) and a guaranteed demand (protein).

Common flies (*Musca domestica*) and "black soldier flies" (*Hermetia illucens*) quickly transform biological waste. The abundance of nutrients in these streams of waste stimulates flies to quickly generate eggs. A fly egg farm produces the trillions of eggs required to start the process. When the eggs hatch—a process that takes three days—they produce protein-rich larvae. This high concentration of protein requires an abundant source of protein which is transformed and sanitized; this is the most critical component of the process. The larvae's digestive track provides a shift in acidity that does not permit any bacteria or viruses to survive. Under the right circumstance, the fly larvae mature in ten days. A new generation of flies is born five days after that. The flies live for some three weeks while they concentrate on mating and finding a suitable place to lay their eggs. One has to time the process carefully or swarms of flies will control the environment.

Biologically, insects are the most efficient animals. They need two kilograms of food to generate one kilogram of insect body weight. Cows, for example, require at least eight kilograms of feed to produce one kilogram of weight gain. From the breaking of the egg, flies can increase their weight 200 times in only ten days. Even a chicken with a selected obesity gene and a diet of superfood cannot match this performance. Insects are efficient in converting food because they are a cold-blooded species with an exceptional digestive system, and they don't need energy to regulate their body temperatures.

Here's what the productivity of fly larvae means in the context of Argentina: the country slaughters ten million cows annually for meat production; the average weight of a cow is 1,000 kilograms; and the after-slaughter waste is about 50 percent, or 500 kilograms. This means that the meat processing industry produces ten million cows x 500 kilograms = five million tons of waste every year. Insects can convert this waste into 2.5 million tons of larvae body weight of which 60 percent—or 1.5 million tons—is protein.

There are, of course, alternative uses for this pile of fat, blood, brains, and lungs. Today, much of that waste is converted into pet food, but even though dog and cat food are sold at premium prices, the income is not attractive as the cost of taste and odor enhancers to make pets eat what most humans do not is high. The quest for competitiveness these days relies not on "being the cheapest," but rather, on "the capability to generate the most value." It is within this context that Argentina has an exceptional opportunity to build a new industry.

Today, Argentina produces an estimated 7.3 million tons of protein per year. Only the conversion of existing waste streams in the meat industry through the conversion of offal at the abattoirs adds 20 percent to this total. Argentina has, of course, much more organic waste than the byproduct of blood and brains from meat processing it is able to convert. Combining various sources of organic waste—including vegetable sources—further increases the larvae's nutritional value.

The larvae fetch a premium price since they have a higher amount of healthy Omega-3 fatty acids when compared to fish. They are also rich in fiber and micronutrients, such as copper, iron, magnesium, phosphorus, manganese, selenium, calcium, zinc, and vitamins A, B2, and C.

The larvae could be sold live as a quality feed for fish and poultry, or they could be dehydrated to create a consistent substitute for fishmeal. Feeding insects to local poultry requires tight supply chain management since even a few hours delay when delivering could cause an annoying fly problem. The fresh supply, however, has an additional advantage in that the larvae contain 50 percent water. Chicken that currently gets dry feed to save on transportation costs will also require large amounts of drinking water. A fresh supply of larvae will solve a major health challenge for chicken farms—preventing the chickens from polluting their drinking water with their feces. This problem has led to the need to add antibiotics to control the cycle of diseases terrifying the sector.

The impact on the global scale is tremendous. Each ton of larvae can replace a ton of fish that is caught only to feed other fish. Salmon, for example, devour three kilograms of sardines or anchovies to produce one kilogram of their popular, orange flesh. This means that larvae production can relieve the pressure on South America as the biggest producer of anchovies in the world. This pressure is reflected in the recent, sharp increase in the price of fishmeal which has risen from 1,000 to 1,500 and 2,000 dollars per ton.

Fly larvae can replace 25 to 100 percent of the soy and fishmeal currently fed to animals. This fact has a huge, potential, environmental impact. The world market for animal feed is about one billion tons with a value of 400 billion dollars. Eighty percent of that market—800 million tons— is served with soybeans. To produce that amount of soy, a landmass of almost 2.5 million square kilometers—about the size of Argentina and four times the size of France—is needed. The production of soybeans also requires 1,700 trillion liters of water annually, enough to provide 59 (!) billion people their daily requirement of 80 liters per person, 365 days a year. In other words, the use of larvae to convert existing waste can solve drinking water challenges in the world, as well. Argentina is increasingly suffering from water shortages, as well, and this strategic option will allow it to pursue a systemic approach.

There is, however, more demand for fly larvae. They are superior "sanitization machines" when converting waste vulnerable to bacterial attacks. This, in the first place, is very helpful when cleaning up pollution caused by the waste generated by slaughterhouses. The same quality makes larvae saliva effective in the treatment of wounds in hospitals that demonstrate an increasing ineffectiveness where antibiotics are concerned. In the past twenty years, larvae have frequently been used to treat diabetic lesions and reduce the risk of amputation, reviving an ancient tradition. The field of diabetes offers a vast market: the United States spent 20 billion dollars on diabetic wound treatment in 2013. There are currently 29 million Americans with diabetes, and by some estimates, one in three Americans will suffer from this disease by 2050.

It is furthermore possible to extract oils and lipids from the larvae which can be used in the cosmetics industry. Finally, the remains of the food left behind by the larvae can be used as fertilizer. All of these opportunities are known, documented, and proven as a business model.

Given the massive potential of fly larvae, especially in nations with a rich agriculture, it does not surprise that in 2015, following FAO recommendations, the European Union incorporated insects as a new source of protein in the food chain of animals and humans. One of the leaders in this new, emerging field is AgriProtein from South Africa. With support from the Australian government, this company is setting up 20 fly farms to convert 1.8 million tons of organic waste. With an army of 8.5 billion flies, the farms will have an annual output of 5,000 tons of larvae feed, 2,000 tons of maggot oil, and leftovers providing high-value compost. In another example of the beneficial impact of larvae production, AgriProtein is also assisting local communities in South Africa that lack sewage systems to treat human waste through larvae-based systems. This approach will create a sewage service that will pay for itself.

It is easy to forecast that in the next ten years there will be lucrative opportunities in the world for some 500 production companies like AgroProtein. These factories could have a combined output of between 1,000 and 5,000 tons a day generating—at 2,000 dollars a ton—between two and ten million dollars in revenue daily and between 250,000 and 500,000 jobs.

There is huge potential in this, and Argentina is well-positioned to become an early leader in this lucrative field. To begin with, the country has some 650 slaughterhouses, many of which are currently a source of substantial environmental pollution. Blood spills into rivers cause unhealthy levels of phosphorous and nitrogen, but larvae production will clean up this mess while providing an attractive, additional income to the non-lucrative industry, such as meat processing. The waste from a small slaughterhouse can generate up to 375

Plan A

kilos of larvae per week—or 20 tons a year—with one kilo of fly eggs. This would mean an additional, annual income of 40,000 dollars. Depending on the processing capacity, a larvae production plant—built close to a meat-processing facility to save transportation costs—requires an investment between four and 12 million dollars. This investment is lower when the plant only produces live larvae, as an installation to create dry feed will add to the cost.

The development of larvae cultivation does not require much land space. It will reduce pollution and save precious resources. Apart from the initial investment, the raw material is free. Whenever the operating expenses are low, a strategic shift sets the direction of the market, changing the rules of the game. Cultivating larvae will generate economic development and create new jobs within a sustainable environmental framework. It is the kind of initiative for which every government looks.

The Transformation of Argentina's Economy

Plan A

Clustering slaughter houses with feed

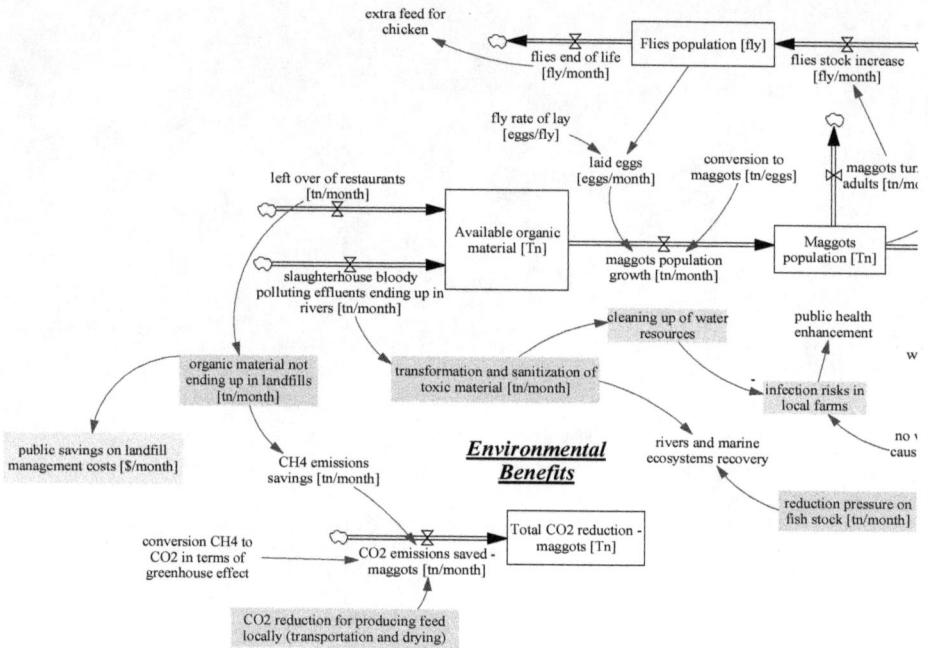

extra feed for chicken

flies end of life [fly/month]

Flies population [fly]

flies stock increase [fly/month]

fly rate of lay [eggs/fly]

laid eggs [eggs/month]

conversion to maggots [tn/eggs]

maggots tur adults [tn/m

left over of restaurants [tn/month]

Available organic material [Tn]

maggots population growth [tn/month]

Maggots population [Tn]

slaughterhouse bloody polluting effluents ending up in rivers [tn/month]

cleaning up of water resources

public health enhancement

w

organic material not ending up in landfills [tn/month]

transformation and sanitization of toxic material [tn/month]

infection risks in local farms

no
caus

public savings on landfill management costs [$/month]

CH4 emissions savings [tn/month]

Environmental Benefits

rivers and marine ecosystems recovery

reduction pressure on fish stock [tn/month]

conversion CH4 to CO2 in terms of greenhouse effect

CO2 emissions saved - maggots [tn/month]

Total CO2 reduction - maggots [Tn]

CO2 reduction for producing feed locally (transportation and drying)

larval therapy
development

afforable treatment
for diabetis

healing agent

direct jobs created
[jobs]

oils and lipids for the
cosmetics industry

reduced risk of
illnesses

*Community
resilience*

byproducts
generated

organic
fertilizer

hunger and poverty
reduction

maggots price
[$/tn]

ning
onth]

dried maggots for
export [tn/month]

healthy human food rich in
micronutrients and Omega3

sales fresh maggots
[$/month]

+ slaughterhouse
competitiveness

maggots harvesting
[tn/month]

fresh proteic food for local
aquaculture and poultry
[tn/month]

new money circulating in the
local economy - maggots
[$/month]

*Multiplier effect on
the local economy*

ater saved in the farms thanks
to the high water content in
fresh maggots

+

water contamination
ed by chickens' feces

volume of soya meal
substituted [tn/month]

+ exports of soya and
+ fishmeal [$/month]

<public savings on landfill
management costs
[$/month]>

volume of fish meal
substituted [tn/month]

Fable 2

Maggot spit

The power of flies is their unparalleled productivity, however, as with all proposals for investment inspired by the Blue Economy, there is more to it than a simple improvement in output. The transformation of biological waste from plant to animal protein to a product with a higher value is only the beginning of a process that takes the project beyond expectations. The fact that slaughterhouse waste, which all too often contaminates rivers and endangers public health, can be converted to protein on an industrial scale is a breakthrough, but the extraction of saliva permitting the control of diabetic ulcers takes the business to a new level, serving society with what is available.

A covey of quails is foraging in an area infested with flies.

"We are having one of the greatest luncheons ever," giggles one quail.

"Indeed. It is so strange that people simply don't like flies."

"Well, people do not like what they don't understand. Flies are like food factories."

"Yes, for us that is true, but people could never imagine eating maggots."

"Well, they do like our tiny and super-nutritious eggs, but when they see maggots crawling around in waste, they put up their noses and shut their eyes."

"Oh, these chubby maggots are simply the tastiest I have had in a long time. We had better hurry, or they will turn into flies. And to be honest, flies simply are not as tasty."

"I agree, but there is nothing on earth that makes protein faster than these tiny fly eggs once they turn into maggots. Can you imagine? Providing they have enough food, one kilogram of fly eggs turns into more than 300 kilograms of wonderful, protein-rich food within just three days!"

"No one can do better. I believe not even algae, mushrooms, or bacteria match this performance! Did you know these maggots have a very special saliva?"

"What is so special about their spit?"

"It helps heal wounds."

"Really? How does that work?"

"Well, it helps cells to grow while it cleans wounds of dead tissue."

"That sounds great, but would you want maggots crawling all over your body?"

"Perhaps, if I had no other choice. If a wound does not heal, the doctor may have to amputate, and that would mean losing a foot or a limb."

"Why don't they milk the spit?"

"Hmm, extracting spit…now, that sounds like a challenge."

"Hey, what happens to you when your head goes underwater at the beach?"

"Nothing. I take care to close my beak and breathe out through my nose."

"But if a big wave surprises you, turning you upside down and you gulp a lot of salt water, then what?"

"Ugh! You know I would throw up."

Plan A

"That's what I thought. So, let us put the maggots in salt water and skim their spit. It may not sound appetizing, but it will certainly provide relief for people with open wounds."

"You are right. People should realize that time alone does not heal all wounds, and that a maggot can certainly offer some help."

...and it has only just begun!

Chapter 2

Re-energizing
the local economy with mushrooms

Governments want to serve the needs of their citizens, provide economic and social opportunities, and support public health. All of these objectives require healthy, local economies that provide local jobs. The stimulation of local economies begins by focusing on the basic—or local—needs of people: water, food, housing, health, energy, and education.

Many people the world over are desperately looking for ways to make money. Many people think that you need money and resources to make money, so they feel frustrated, powerless, and caught in a vicious circle while they look to the government for support. They don't see the potential wealth in the environment around them. There are always, however, accessible, local, and available resources, even when nothing seems available. This is the key: discover what you have, and what it is useful for. The best solutions to local problems emerge in local opportunities, and with it, a sense of empowerment and the strengthening of the belief that the community has the capacity to progress.

As we know, Argentina is a major, global, food producer.

Plan A

People in many countries benefit from Argentina's extraordinary efforts on a daily basis, however, the success of the country, in many ways, fails to reach everyone in the local communities.

Argentina has a major opportunity to address this painful reality in an efficient, low-cost way, using biomass, something the country has in abundance. Argentina can follow the example of an inspiring story from some 20 years ago that has since been replicated some 5,000 times around the world, changing the lives of thousands of people. It's also a story that Argentine coffee drinkers will love.

At the age of 11, Chido Govera was an orphan in rural Zimbabwe. She never knew her father, and her mother had died from AIDS when she was seven. Chido took care of her blind grandmother and her younger brother, trying to find food and water while she was being physically abused by members of her extended family. A relative suggested she marry a 50-year-old man to escape her life of poverty and abuse, but the 11-year-old chose a different path and went to the local church. There, she was introduced to a project developed by Zero-emissions Research and Initiatives (ZERI), a global network of scientists and entrepreneurs seeking solutions to the world's problems. ZERI had developed a method inspired by Professor Shuting Chang, a Chinese scientist credited with farming innovations in China, to cultivate mushrooms on grass clippings, coffee grounds, corn cobs, and water hyacinth—resources, "waste," that is within everyone's reach. ZERI scientists had discovered that 100 pounds of water hyacinths could produce as many as 240 pounds of tropical mushrooms. Some mushroom varieties contain about 25 percent of the protein found in meat and all essential amino acids needed by human beings, giving them a high nutritional value.

The logic of the project in Zimbabwe was straightforward: the first flush of mushrooms could be harvested within a few weeks, and this would provide food, nutrition security, and income for orphaned girls who would subsequently be able to "refuse" abuse. Chido was among 15 girls between the ages of 11 and 14 selected by the church to learn how to take their future in their own hands. The results were amazing; the transformation of the girls dramatic. They matured in just a few weeks with smiles on their faces. A simple biological process had led to fundamental societal transformation.

Twenty years later, there are an estimated 5,000 mushroom businesses in the world. These are not just small businesses to lift people out of poverty. Setas is a large mushroom farm in Colombia, generating 17 million dollars annually by growing mushrooms on waste generated by coffee and sugar cane production. Two college graduates from the Haas School of Business at Berkeley University, Alejandro Velez and Nikhil Arora, started a mushroom business in the San Francisco Bay Area in 2007. Today, their company, Back to the Roots, has grown into a business with 50 employees.

If all coffee waste—from the farming leftovers to the grounds from cafes around the world—was used to farm mushrooms, the world could produce an additional 16 million tons of food and animal feed per year. This is only on coffee! It would not require the use of any additional land, and we would only *use what we already have today.* Organic waste, biomass from agriculture-rich in fibers, should never be left to rot or used for compost. Although composting is good, it does not generate real jobs. Apart from lost income opportunities, rotting generates methane gas, a greenhouse gas 21 times more harmful than CO_2.

Argentina generates an estimated 18 million tons of plant waste every year. On average, 50 percent of that biomass can be converted into mushrooms. That is nine million tons of mushrooms with a market value of 1,000 dollars per ton, a potential value of nine billion dollars per year—income that can be created simply by using what Argentina, as a major food producer, has in abundance.

A potential annual production of nine million tons of mushrooms per year translates to 200 kilograms of mushrooms per Argentinian per year. The average world citizen eats four kilograms of mushrooms per year, with Hong Kong leading the global consumption at 14 kilograms per person per year. Two hundred kilograms per Argentinian goes beyond the country's needs, however, the point is that a simple addition to Argentina's agricultural production would easily solve the challenges the country faces regarding malnutrition, as mushrooms provide a full range of essential amino acids, the essential building blocks of life.

But we are told over and over again that the Argentinians are carnivores. They love meat. They are not going to eat mushrooms. This may be true. It's definitely true that there is a worldwide health trend toward a more plant-based diet, and mushrooms can and will play a major role in that trend, not just as fresh produce, but also as an ingredient to use in veggie burgers, sauces, soups, broths, etc. On top of that, mushrooms provide good feed for animals. The substrate used for farming mushrooms has been digested by the fungi's enzymes, which have further enriched it with more amino acids, turning something that was not previously edible into something desirable for animals.

The cultivation of mushrooms can help Argentina meet its domestic, nutrition challenges. It will also add a new dimension to Argentina's export portfolio as one of the top ten global food producers. Mushrooms are a rapidly growing market: between 1997 and 2012, global consumption grew by 400 percent, illustrating patterns in a changing diet, even amongst the world's most ardent carnivores. Annual worldwide growth continues in the double digits, and the current world market value of traded edible mushrooms is 25 billion dollars. Based on the biomass that Argentina currently produces, the country has the opportunity to capture more than 30 percent of the world market.

How would it do that?

Mushroom cultivation is very different from major crops like soy and corn as it is much more labor-intensive. There is also a major difference in cash flow generation. If you plant soy, you need to prepare the land and turn the soil to remove competing growth before you plant, and you can only harvest three months later. Mushrooms can be seeded in a locally available substrate and harvested in two weeks, with more to be collected in the following weeks. More work is a good thing for Argentina which, like most nations with economies in transition, faces the challenge of too many people leaving rural areas with the hope of finding work in cities. The new and labor-intensive work of mushroom cultivation supports re-ruralization and comes at a good price: processed mushrooms sell for 1,000 dollars per ton compared to soy with the price of 300 dollars per ton. Argentina is the largest producer of its peers in the Southern Hemisphere, and the fifth largest apple exporter in the world. In the provinces of Rio Negro and Neuquen, each tree needs to be pruned, leaving an extraordinary amount of hardwood behind, ideal for mushroom farming. This market segment should not be considered a commodity—mushrooms should be produced with the added value of ensuring that more new jobs are generated than can ever be imagined today.

Intensive farming crops, like soy, use large and expensive machinery and equipment which requires large investments that drive the concentration of power. As a result, the return on wealth and employment isn't easily distributed throughout the economy. Mushroom cultivation creates jobs, for example, over the past decade, the introduction of shiitake mushroom cultivation has created 20,000 jobs in the United States. This economic success surfs on the trend of changing appetites. Names like shiitake, enoki, oyster, and portobello were not familiar until recently, but can be found in all supermarkets today.

In the past, it was not easy to enter the mushroom-farming market. Cultivation was energy-intensive because the standard methodology for farming prescribed sterilization. The costs involved in sterilization—steaming the substrate for hours— made up some 50 percent of the production. It also required access to an energy infrastructure, which made starting a mushroom farm complex.

New techniques demonstrated around the world make it possible to efficiently grow mushrooms without the need for sterilization, allowing for small-scale cultivation. As in the story of Zimbabwe, it starts with one initiative which is followed by another. The process is easy and requires so little investment, it has the ability to spread like wildfire. Anyone can grow his first mushroom harvest of 100 kilos in two weeks with an investment of 500 dollars. Within two months, the initial investment will be earned back while they scale their production, step-by-step, to perhaps as much as 1,000 kilos per day. Larger operations that start with a production of 1,000 kilos per day require a bigger investment of about 50,000 dollars.

Raw material is available everywhere: the sawdust from the sawmill in Tierra del Fuego; the waste from the soy processing mill in Santa Fe; or the clippings from fruit trees in Río Negro, Neuquén, Mendoza, and La Pampa y San Juan. There is a massive opportunity to scale mushroom farming through the farmers' networks of Argentina. Argentina can become a leading mushroom producer, next to China, as the most successful mushroom-farming nation in the world. The leading centers of mushroom-farming in China employ 100,000 people in areas equal to the size of San Francisco. The precondition is that the raw materials exist in abundance. There is no doubt that Argentina has multiple centers with an abundance of biomass ready for conversion into substrate.

Argentina can launch this new mission with the first

generation of 100 mushroom-cultivating enterprises, not just in rural areas, but in cities as well. Coffee grounds provide an ideal substrate for growing mushrooms, and there is no shortage of coffee shops in Argentina—it is part of their culture. Chido Govera came to Buenos Aires to share her experience, and Julien Laurençon from the Comunidad Huerta has 5,000 farmers who are dedicated to the production of fruits and vegetables, ready to embark on the farming of mushrooms. They have an established network of clients based on the proven business model of community-supported agriculture and will provide the training for the first 100 mushroom farmers.

Mushroom farming means using waste with hardly any value to create a lot of value. Mushrooms are 50 times more valuable than compost. In fact, the compost that mushrooms leave behind after harvesting is of a higher quality because it has been enriched with nutrients from micro-organisms. Mushroom cultivation fights malnutrition and global warming, and it has the potential to create hundreds of thousands of jobs in a low-capital-cost, decentralized way. Finally, mushroom farming fills a gap in natural cycles. Farms grow food; the organic waste from the farms is used to grow mushrooms; what is left after the mushroom harvest is the perfect feed for animals; and the animal manure is a high-quality fertilizer.

It's a natural cycle where value—income, nutrition, and employment—is added at each step. Adding value means building local communities and economies. This is what governments want to do.

The Transformation of Argentina's Economy

Plan A

Clustering mushrooms with coffee

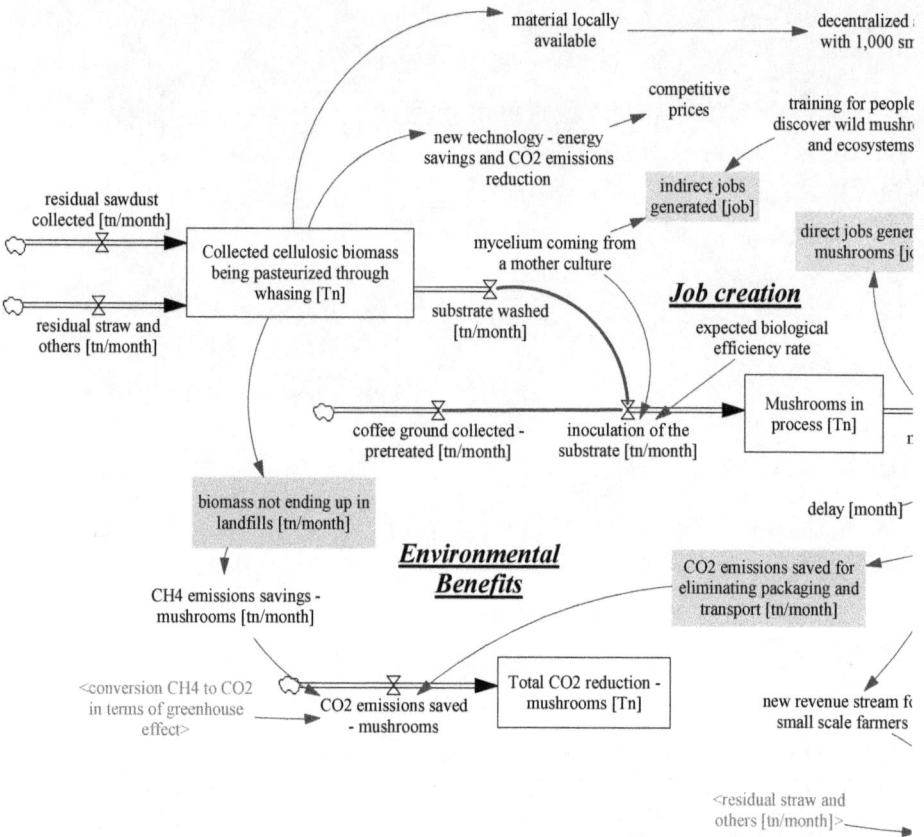

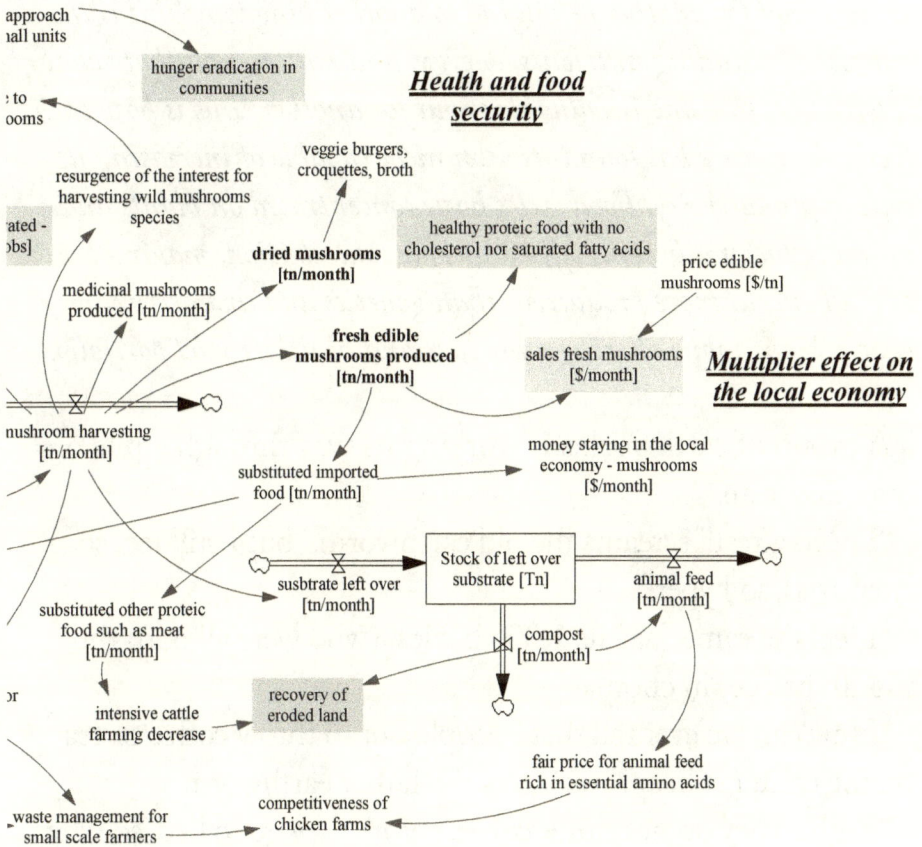

approach
ıall units

hunger eradication in
communities

Health and food securrity

: to
ooms

resurgence of the interest for
harvesting wild mushrooms
species

veggie burgers,
croquettes, broth

ated -
ɔbs]

dried mushrooms
[tn/month]

healthy proteic food with no
cholesterol nor saturated fatty acids

price edible
mushrooms [$/tn]

medicinal mushrooms
produced [tn/month]

fresh edible
mushrooms produced
[tn/month]

sales fresh mushrooms
[$/month]

Multiplier effect on the local economy

nushroom harvesting
[tn/month]

substituted imported
food [tn/month]

money staying in the local
economy - mushrooms
[$/month]

Stock of left over
substrate [Tn]

susbtrate left over
[tn/month]

animal feed
[tn/month]

substituted other proteic
food such as meat
[tn/month]

compost
[tn/month]

ɔr

recovery of
eroded land

intensive cattle
farming decrease

fair price for animal feed
rich in essential amino acids

waste management for
small scale farmers

competitiveness of
chicken farms

Plan A

Shiitake love caffeine

Organic waste should never be called "waste." The waste of one is always food for another belonging to another kingdom. This is the marvel of cascading nutrients, energy, and matter, and that what is left over from one is valuable input for another. This is how each species in nature has found its own niche capable of increasing its cycle of productivity. Food cycles have concentrated on plants and animals, but mushrooms offer a unique contribution, making the overall output more productive than genetics and chemistry can ever achieve while offering a broader and healthier food portfolio.

A group of earthworms is working its way through a pile of organic waste.

"I need a rest!" screams the old earthworm, "but I still feel so energized, so hyper!"

"I feel the same," say its 1,000 babies (who were all born the month before) in chorus.

"How can we ever tell these people not to throw coffee or tea on the compost heap?" whispers the father earthworm.

"Right. They do not drink coffee before they go to bed, so why do they throw all of this caffeine at us where we make our beds? I am stressed out!" says the youngest of the colony.

"Well, well, what do I hear?" wonders the shiitake mushroom. "Are you all suffering from too much caffeine?"

"You see, these people have learned they cannot feed it to cattle, even when it is rich in nutrients like protein or the cows get stressed and give less milk."

"And since you do not give milk, people do not know that it bothers you?"

"'Well, they do not know what we are going through, but having to eat and digest your own weight every day is quite a job."

"I can help," says the shiitake, "I can grow here and get my energy from the caffeine."

"What? You do not get stressed from caffeine?"

"No. Actually, the more caffeine there is, the better it is for me. I use it to grow and convert the caffeine into food for others. You will be able to eat all of the organic waste and not get stressed. Even the cattle would be able to eat it!"

"Wow! That would be great, but how does this work?"

"You are an animal, coffee is a plant, and I am a fungus—we belong to three different kingdoms."

"I know that even though we do not have legs and we are blind, we belong to the Animal Kingdom," says the earthworm.

"So, animals suffer from caffeine, but some fungi can live in any fiber, even if it includes caffeine. Then, we produce waste rich in protein without the caffeine."

"That is great! You fungi make the food we can eat; we earthworms prepare food for plants; and the cattle eats the plants! Everyone works together, and no one gets stressed."

... and it has only just begun!

Plan A

Chapter 3

The power of fish, pigs, goats, milk and cheese

Argentina leads the world in two statistics: the country cultivates the highest percentage of genetically modified organisms (GMO)) crops, and it is also the largest consumer per capita of pesticides and herbicides. These are interesting facts, considering the introduction of GMOs was meant to decrease—if not eradicate—the use of pesticides and herbicides.

Beneath this apparent contradiction lies the core principle of modern industrial agriculture: standardization. The prevailing logic is that whatever we can standardize we can measure and control—the same ingredients, fed into the same process, produce the same outcome. Since the Industrial Revolution, the system has worked well for factories producing the same products all the time. In the past century, we have applied this logic to the assembly of cars, computers, and televisions with success—this is where robots come in handy. We have, however, applied the same industrial model to the way we grow and produce food. That is, we have applied our industrial model to nature. The logic of the supply chain of steel to wheel has been applied to soil and seeds and from farm to fork. As a result, today's whole world population eats basically five plants: wheat, rice, corn, soy, and palm; drinks one type of milk (from the cow, of course); and eats meat from three animals: pigs, chickens, and cows.

Around the world, a few corporations control the five crops and the meat and dairy industries who have perfected the complete chain from genetics to processing and delivery to the consumer. Everything is cultivated in nearly the same way—from the planting of the seeds and the handling of the artificial nutrients in the soil to the processing of the harvest. Farmers have been increasingly transformed into laborers supplying a piece of land and following precise instructions to ensure the predictability demanded by food multinationals. The reason is simple: the corn flakes you buy in Paris need to taste the same as the corn flakes you buy in Buenos Aires, and the nutritional labels need to be the same. It is all about predictability and eradicating risk in a very fragile system. The same applies to the color of salmon or pork bellies and most other produce and animal protein you buy in the supermarket, wherever you are. If we left it to nature, food from different places would always look and taste differently.

Universally identical red ketchup, golden corn flakes, and pink salmon are the results of our attempts to force biology to become predictable, reducing the business risk and increasing returns on the investments of food multinationals. We have strived to master nature with monocultures and GMOs. It is a mission destined to be a temporary success because nature always adapts and responds. Bacteria swiftly create new varieties that undo the human genius. This is why Argentina consumes so many agricultural chemicals despite heavy investments in GMOs.

Industrial farming has another important, negative side effect: it has significantly decreased population density in the countryside. Somehow, economists have equated the decrease in employment in the primary sector with progress. This is certainly not a sign of development and modernization if the price society pays is the loss of nutritious food, the dramatic increase of diabetes and obesity, and the disintegration of rural communities. At the same time, the ongoing trend of urbanization challenges the ability of the government to meet and satisfy the basic needs of the population. Poverty is increasing, and personal security is decreasing. Ultimately, industrial farming will threaten the economic and social stability of Argentina. It is, therefore, critical that the country seeks the development of local, integrated and sustainable economic alternatives.

Industrialized farming goes against the logic of five billion years of evolution in which fauna and flora have embarked on a never-ending quest to evolve and diversify. Monocultures create disease because they "invite" pests, and an explosive growth of wild plants—let us not call these weeds—are keen to fill the ecological niche left open and unused. Monoculture farming, driven by the desire to master nature, contains this inherent flaw: it ignores the way nature works. Nature uses its "five kingdoms"—bacteria, algae, fungi, plants, and animals—

to preserve diversity, balance, and hygiene, promoting life and building up social capital with resilience. Nature continuously shifts action, matter, energy, and nutrition from one kingdom to another. A virus that attacks a pig has no effect on a plant. A virus that eradicates shrimp farms or undermines banana plantations is irrelevant in a spirulina production pond. None of these viruses can survive when they get into the bacterial environment of, for instance, a biogas digester in the presence of very little oxygen and the abundant production of methane.

Nonetheless, if the virus survives the digester, it cannot survive in the high pH environment of an algae pond. The biodiversity that is the power of nature is not made only from different species, but also from different families creating different living conditions inside particular niches within the ecosystem. With "environmental shifts" of dynamic life conditions—including acid and alkaline, aerobic and non-aerobic, high and low temperatures, with or without magnetism, inside or outside a cell, high or low water surface tension—nature provides conditions to enhance all aspects of life. Nature has no need for weed, fungal, or pest control since the system continuously responds and adapts in diverse ways, and improper imbalances are quickly corrected without the need for toxic external support.

The agriculture of the future is not GMO-based; it will be modeled on nature, and Argentina can be an early pioneer and world-leader of this approach. Integrated farming based on the laws of nature is superior in productivity. It generates more value and jobs and permits nature to regenerate its soil.

Sustainable rural communities—with full access to all of the resources of the information society—that produce food and energy locally can offer opportunities for employment and entrepreneurship and revitalize rural areas.

Argentina, with its large expanse of fertile and flat land and with an abundance of water, is ideally positioned to transform industrial agriculture into integrated biosystems that turn waste into food and fuel for the whole country. Food and fuel production increases and new possibilities for value-creation arise. In integrated biosystems, organic molecules can cycle indefinitely while continuously regenerating nature.

Given the challenges of Argentina's urban centers, it may be tempting to try to implement new agricultural solutions in places where the need is the highest. It is, however, a typical flaw of industrial thinking to look for solutions where we want them to be, rather than look in the best places and where they are available. Integrated farming does not flourish in large-scale environments, but in a distributed system with different forms and scales of production. Argentina has a rich potential to produce food and fuel from biomass that is spread out across the vast country. The following example illustrates how a focus on local resources can generate an abundance of value.

Cluster 1: beer, pigs, fish, energy, and rice

Twenty years ago, in Fiji, ZERI first applied this approach in an effort to dramatically increase output. In cooperation with Professor George Chan, we set out to demonstrate the performance of food production based on traditional Chinese systems. Chan, who was trained at Imperial College of London, had a career as the water engineer in his birth town of Port Louis, Mauritius, and as an environmental engineer for the United States Environmental Protection Agency (EPA) in the Pacific. After his early retirement, he decided to study traditional farming in his ancestral homeland of China.

The islands of Fiji enjoy abundance, but the soil is considered poor, and hardly anything grows in the slippery clay. Chan decided to focus on Montfort Boys Town, a technical school located outside the capital city of Suva. There, students learned how to farm fish in an attempt to make the school self-sufficient in food. The school was following the "scientific" technique based on the fattening of fingerlings of an imported species (tilapia) with imported feed in shallow ponds. The success was measured in tons of output, not in the concentration of nutrition. It is a very inefficient—and expensive—system that works only with the free labor of the students!

Chan set out to demonstrate that it is possible to farm fish without having to buy feed for the fish because—as he argued—nowhere in nature are fish artificially fed. The first step was to deepen the one- or two-foot-deep shallow ponds to ten feet. Chan used a traditional, efficient technique, deepening the ponds some four feet, using the excavated earth to build four-foot-high dikes around the ponds. The next step was to gather seven types of fish. Chan was keen on having fish that live at each trophic level—some like to eat the grass on the top, some like to dredge for food on the bottom, and there is a variety of food for different fish in between—like zoo- and phytoplankton, benthos, and undigested food from other fish. It was quite surprising how precise different species occupied each niche, and how a 3D model of fish farming unfolded where the 30,000 square foot pond turned into a 350,000 cubic foot pond with a diverse and secure food supply. The output had increased by a factor 15, with seven species instead of only one in a pond that had expanded from two to ten feet deep. Traditional agricultural economists would consider this improved output impossible to achieve. However, the result can be easily explained and understood when one realizes that the productive system incorporates a third dimension.

Still, the fish had to be fed at a substantial cost. Chan began planning to eliminate these expenses with a mushroom farm using grains from a local beer producer located a few miles from the school. He also started a piggery for which the pigs were bought locally as one-month-old weaners and fed the spent substrate after harvesting the mushrooms. The pigs were trained to go in the corner and keep the pen clean within a few days, a relief for anyone working on the farm since the least pleasant job would most likely be the brushing of pig excrement into a drop hole feeding the fermenter. This digester produced biogas used to sterilize the mushroom substrate. The slurry from the digester was further mineralized in algae ponds, and the beta-carotene-rich algae that naturally grew was used as a feed additive for the pigs. The algae oxidized the water even further, increasing the pH, allowing for the cultivation and daily harvesting of spirulina. The alkaline water full of minerals in the algae pond turned out to be the ideal feed for benthos, zooplankton, and phytoplankton, which provided the ideal feed for the fish which were also fed daily cut grass growing in the quality topsoil used to create dikes around the pond. The water became so rich in nutrients that a few floating platforms were added to farm rice, and the excess water was used to irrigate the clay-like land around the pond that provided at least two harvests a year but which had once been unfit to farm.

In a year, Chan had created an integrated ecosystem where each step generated revenue while the fish were farmed without having to buy feed. The only investment had been the creation of two piggeries, hosting, in total, 240 pigs per year. The revenue per hectare increased to US$15,000, an income level unheard of in the world of farming. The Fiji experiment showed how animal protein—pigs and seven types of fish—could be produced while harvesting starch-and carbohydrate-rich plants, algae abundant in beta carotene, and a total of 12 sources of food from the same land. This integrated biosystems approach has the highest efficiency in terms of output, provides the best revenues for farmers, and is independent from chemical input because of the protection provided by the five kingdoms. The Fiji case demonstrates the way to food security, surpasses any GMO project in terms of efficiency, yields by a multiple, and can be replicated in many different places, including urban environments. It also embraces the diversity of all kingdoms and as much diversity as possible within each species as well.

Several regions of Argentina have an abundance of water. In these regions, fish farms have been created that have achieved a level of productivity and revenue comparable to where Montfort Boys Town stood at the outset of the transformation program. This means that there is a great investment opportunity in regions like the province of Entre Rios. A field visit to the locality of Avigdor demonstrated that the soil fertility and biodiversity of this region allows for extraordinary opportunities for organic food production in integrated systems that can attract young entrepreneurs. The investment costs are limited to excavation and labor and are estimated at 6,000 to 10,000 dollars per hectare. After this initial investment, ongoing revenue is guaranteed at a low, operational expense, offering returns in excess of 50 percent.

Cluster 2: Chickens, pigs, sausages, quality nutrition, and land value

Argentina already produces high-quality, grass-fed meat without adding antibiotics. There is a great opportunity to add even more value to the meat industry, based on a model developed in Germany. German meat producer, Karl Ludwig Schweisfurth, discovered the limitations of the standardization of industrial farming in his own way. Schweisfurth was the owner of Herta, one of the world's largest sausage companies. His father started the business in 1902, and after his training at American meat-packing plants, he introduced the same logic of economies of scale and cost-cutting drives to become the largest meat-processing company in Europe. Every week, the company transformed 25,000 pigs and 5,000 cows—1.5 million animals each year— into sausages and cuts of meat. Herta was profitable, and it

was poised for growth worldwide because of the excellent
technical performance and strong German brand that stood
tall in terms of quality, but Schweisfurth's children didn't like
the business. In fact, his two sons and one daughter rejected
the very business model on which the wealth of the family
had been built. One son became interested in agro-ecology,
and the other became a pioneer of health food stores in
Germany.

Then, Karl Ludwig Schweisfurth did something of which
very few successful entrepreneurs are capable. Listening to
his children, he radically changed course, selling his business
to Nestlé, and joining his children in a new endeavor
to transform the industry from the bottom up, and the
Herrmannsdorf farm in Glonn outside of Munich was
born. Karl Ludwig and his sons, Karl and Georg, against
a wave of ridicule and critique, created a 250-acre farm
where everything is vertically integrated, just like farming
used to be. They redesigned the business model for food
with its quality measured by the value of nutrition as the
top priority in everything produced. Food-industry experts
balked at the price Herrmannsdorf set out to charge for
its food, which was easily double the price of comparable
products in supermarkets. The arguments were clear from
the start: the food was not comparable pound for pound.
The difference was in the nutritional value. On the basis of
nutrition, Herrmannsdorf meat was cheaper; on the basis of
weight, it was outrageously expensive. What, then, should
the economist opt for: to have cheap food and a high cost
for health care, or to save vast amounts of money by selling

healthy food on the basis of its superior, nutritional content?

Herrmannsdorf demonstrates that the market responds to a business model where the feed is produced locally; chickens and pigs, females and males, roam the land with ducks and goats; where chickens feast on the insects bothering the pigs; and the pigs provide heat for the chickens in the winter. The animals are cared for in double or even triple the time industrial piggeries, or chicken batteries consider competitive. All animals can walk to the boutique-sized slaughterhouse where they spend the night with friends before being sacrificed with great care. Their meat is processed immediately at their body temperature, and nothing is lost. Herrmannsdorf shows that food is—as the Germans say—lebensmittel, a means to live. The processing is carefully undertaken, from the preparation of the soil to the selection of feed for the animals who are chosen from traditional varieties for taste and resilience to weather patterns, and finally to the skills of the butcher and the makers of delicatessen meats that stand out in quality and taste.

The success of the integrated model is based not only on mastering the production and processing of food but also on its distribution. The Schweisfurth family refuses to work with supermarkets and has established its own distribution channel based on the experience and contacts son Georg had in the health food and organic stores sector. The fully integrated and controlled chain—from feed to farm to shop—is extended to their restaurant, hotel, and catering service. Nobody expected the business to succeed, but the business provides so much revenue today it is almost embarrassing. The demand for more comes not just from Germany, but from around the world. Herrmannsdorf has integrated farmers in the region who follow the same logic and ethics, and the farm has supported the start-up of numerous other farms.

Some comment the Herrmannsdorf model is too capital intensive and only for the rich. The counterargument is that Herrmannsdorf delivers much better nutrition, much better value, and therefore, deserves a higher price. Moreover, Herrmannsdorf meat offers such value that one can eat less and still have more nutrition. Pigs reared at the Herrmannsdorf farm have higher levels of beta-carotene, the highly sought-after nutrition making salmon so popular. The presence of this quality nutrient alone offers compensation for the fact the animals are kept a minimum of one year instead of the typical six months. Ultimately, better nutrition contributes to better health, thus leading to savings on health care expenses. Still, there is a challenge for consumers society-wide to make the shift. Arguably, the people who are most in need of more nutritious foods are the ones who can't afford to pay the higher price of Herrmannsdorf sausages.

Argentina has an extraordinary opportunity to add even more value to this core industry through the adoption of the Herrmannsdorf-model. The investment would improve export revenue as well as public health in the country. Apart from the cost of land acquisition (100 hectares), the investment in infrastructure to create a "Herrmannsdorf farm" is estimated at three million dollars, including the slaughterhouse, the processing center, and the nursing site for the chickens and pigs. The income generated on that farm reaches 30 million dollars per year, with a five to eight percent net return, while generating more than 280 full time, well-paid jobs. The real value, however, beyond the sales, is the increase in asset value. A traditional hectare producing 20 tons of protein valued at 350 dollars per ton under ideal conditions only offers a cash entry of 6,000 dollars per year. The integrated farming model generates a multiple of five, reaching 30,000 dollars, which immediately translates into an increased valuation of the land itself.

Re-evaluating Argentina's opportunities from the perspective of integrated farming inspired by the laws of nature with a permanent search for more produce and more cash flow may also lead to different choices. The predominant beef industry may not serve the needs of the country best everywhere. In certain regions, feeding cows with soy may not be the best farming system at all.

Cluster 3: goats, milk, yogurt, organic fruits, and cheese

Twenty years ago, El Hierro, part of the Canary Islands off the coast of Spain, was an island in search of a future. The livestock situation was analyzed and farmers recognized that feeding cows on the island was inefficient. Cows are not native and need additional, imported, feed, especially in the winter season, and the dry land is incapable of producing local hay in volumes warranted by the local supply. This increases costs. Goats, however, stood out as the ideal animals. Canary Island goats are champions in meat and milk production. A renewed focus on goat farming, specifically on the creation of higher-value products, subsequently led to a

Plan A

remarkable economic recovery. Today, El Hierro ranchers get about €2.65 per liter for their goat milk, which is converted into cheese and yogurt. That is ten (!) times more than the subsidized tariff paid for milk by the European Union. The star product is fresh yogurt, served with organic banana and pineapple that is sold locally and on the adjoining islands. The goat business on El Hierro is lucrative and attracts young people from Spain, which suffers from a very high youth unemployment rate. With only 50 goats producing two liters a day, a farmer can make about 100,000 euros per year. The investment for a flock of 50 with a minimum milking and rearing infrastructure requires no more than 18,000 dollars per farm. A processing center for the production of milk, yogurt, cheese, and meat products requires a joint investment of 1.8 million dollars. The expenses are limited, as the feed for the goats is free, and the living costs on the island are much lower than in any other Spanish city. How many young people can imagine such revenue which will tend to increase, provided there are no more than 50 goats in the herd. The reason? Research has demonstrated that goats appreciate care and attention, and when given the proper attention, they reward the rancher with more milk. This limits the natural scale of a healthy, productive ranch.

The El Hierro model was subsequently copied from the Dutch Caribbean island of Bonaire. There, goat milk was turned into ice cream and sold to the many tourists visiting the island on cruise ships. The logic was quick and clear: the cruise ships disembark on the island, leaving their passengers a couple of hours to stroll the avenue of Kralendijk, the

Capital city of Bonaire, and eat an ice-cream. Tourists are willing to pay six American dollars for a Häagen-Dazs, offering the consumer 50 percent of his daily intake of saturated fat, 30 percent of his cholesterol; only 10 to 15 percent of the product is actually milk, and 25 percent is sugar. The local goat herders could sell the same ice cream with sugar cane from the island at least five times cheaper and add flavors from the island no Häagen-Dazs fan would ever encounter.

The examples of El Hierro and Bonaire provide inspiration for the transformation of Rafaela's struggling dairy industry in the capital of the province of Santa Fe. The milk industry suffers from a downward price spiral driven by intense standardization and concentration. The expert team from ZERI Brazil evaluated the challenges with the Williner Company, a leading player in the regional dairy industry, and discovered an interest and willingness to innovate and explore integrated biosystems, including fermenters, microalgae production, and power generation. Brazilian energy company GeoEnergética (Plaenge Group), owned by Fernando and Alexandre Fabian, has already demonstrated the success of this avenue. Anderson Sakuma, the Plaenge scientific expert on bio-energy trained by Prof. George Chan, joined the project team on special assignment and concluded that Argentina has a tremendous future, and he worked out specific investment opportunities.

The situation in Rafaela illustrates the challenges and opportunities for Argentina. As a first step, the country needs to begin mapping all processes used, from planting food to breeding livestock. That process needs to establish where raw materials are used, where waste is generated, and how new value can be generated by (re)directing production cycles from the small dairy producer to the milk processing plants. Argentina needs to know the organic matter existing in the entire production system associated with the production of milk and milk products in detail, and how that organic matter can be used in an integrated way to produce energy, a key strategic issue in Argentina.

Argentina has an abundance of natural resources, hosting 55 million cows, 14 million sheep, four million pigs, 3.5 million goats, and 115 million chickens. Only 20 percent of the animals in the country are fattened in feedlots; 80 percent is still produced extensively due to a great integration with the production of feed. The healthy, high-quality meat production is free from mad cow disease and is good for an annual export value of 1.5 billion dollars.

Nonetheless, integrated farming can vastly improve the output for the country. For instance, the production of milk and meat has traditionally been separate, but if these farming systems were integrated, productivity would increase substantially and add much more value, as income and jobs would be created. This is a critical shift, as the production of milk dropped 11 percent in 2016 because prices fell so low, Argentinian farmers found it impossible to continue to compete.

The cases described in this chapter offer tremendous opportunities for investors to increase the value of Argentinean agriculture. Farming output can increase fivefold while employment triples and margins increase. With an integrated farming approach, existing resources can create an abundance of value to benefit communities across the country. At the same time, this systemic shift will regenerate nature, ensuring generations to come will continue to enjoy Argentina's richness and wealth.

Plan A

Clustering the 5 kingdoms of nature

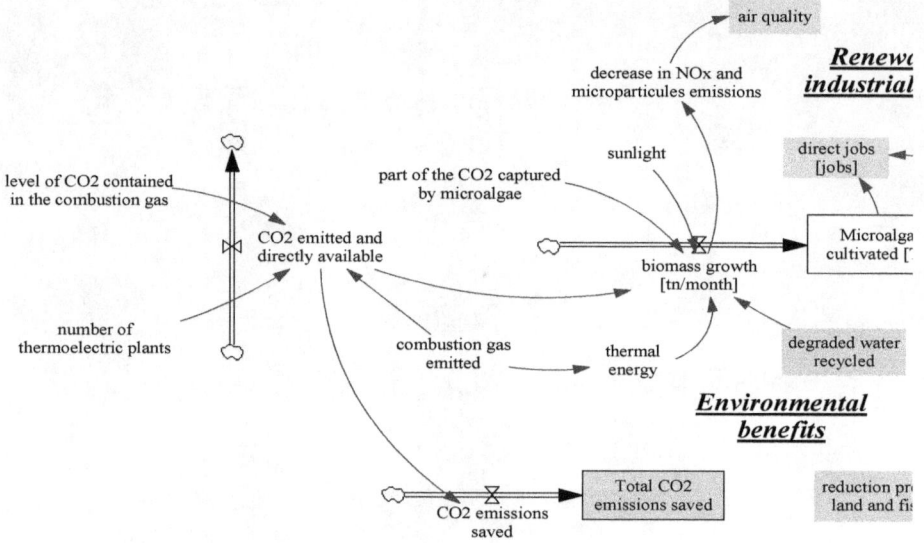

air quality

decrease in NOx and
microparticules emissions

Renew(
industrial

sunlight

direct jobs
[jobs]

level of CO2 contained
in the combustion gas

part of the CO2 captured
by microalgae

CO2 emitted and
directly available

Microalga
cultivated [

biomass growth
[tn/month]

number of
thermoelectric plants

combustion gas
emitted

thermal
energy

degraded water
recycled

Environmental
benefits

Total CO2
emissions saved

reduction pr
land and fis

CO2 emissions
saved

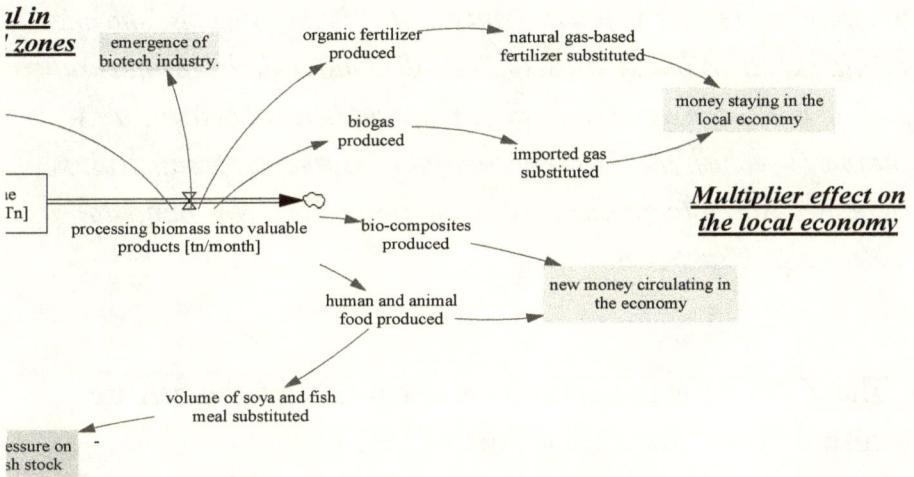

l in
zones

emergence of
biotech industry.

organic fertilizer
produced

natural gas-based
fertilizer substituted

money staying in the
local economy

biogas
produced

imported gas
substituted

e
[n]

processing biomass into valuable
products [tn/month]

bio-composites
produced

Multiplier effect on
the local economy

human and animal
food produced

new money circulating in
the economy

volume of soya and fish
meal substituted

essure on
sh stock

Fable 4

Crabs for dinner

The production of food is reaching new levels of efficiency. The monoculture, aided by genetics and chemistry, is increasingly outpaced by integrated biosystems where the cascading reaches not only high levels of productivity, but it brings surprises no one would expect. What scientists have called autopoiesis, the natural path of evolution and symbiosis, brings additional benefits and income for which there cannot be a plan. However, productivity systems wishing to predict this would never have the chance to welcome such surprises.

The pig and the mushroom are debating why the fish are vanishing from the pond on their farm.

"It must be the birds who come to steal our fish at night," argues the mushroom.

"No, that's not possible—we are very vigilant," defends the pig. "We would have noticed. I wonder if one family of fish isn't eating the other."

"Look," answers the mushroom, "we have seven types of fish here, one for each food level in our three-meter-deep pond. No fish is interested in eating another. It is possible for us to farm fish without having to buy feed for them. Perhaps they got sick and are dying at the bottom of the pond."

"You're right about the levels. The grass-eaters at the top will never bother the bottom feeders. Thanks to the algae, there is a lot of plankton and many tiny snails in the water, which means there's enough food to feed all of the fish.

"I don't understand it. We used to have five times more fish than we have now—what's going on here?"

"I really don't know. Do you think there's a problem with the water?" the mushroom wonders. "I know there are too many solids flowing from your sty, but aren't they caught in the digester's filter?"

"Yes, the solids are, indeed, left behind in the digester. The water for this pond comes from our pigsty. The manure flows into a digester where bacteria purify the water, and the clean water is then returned to nature. Did you know that the digester also creates biogas?"

"That's interesting!" the mushroom replies.

"But if it's not the water, what could the problem be, then?" the pig asks. "We have always had plenty of food sources on this farm. We are providing so much food, even the soil around us, which was considered poor for farming, started to flourish beyond everyone's expectations."

"Those who think poor soil will always remain that way don't think properly," the mushroom replies. Some people thought the water in our pond was polluted as there was too much food in it, but the water from the pond turned out to enrich the soil wonderfully!"

"We still need to do something about our fish disappearing," says the pig.

"So, let's think—where is the excess water from the pond flowing to?" the mushroom asks.

"To the sea."

"And what lives in the coastal zone of the sea, where our

water flows to?" the mushroom wants to know.

"Mangroves."

"Yes, the mangrove swamps are a paradise for shrimp, crabs, seaweed, and algae."

"So, which one of these creatures do you think will move from the sea to the land?" asks the pig.

"Seaweed and algae have no chance, and shrimp can hardly walk," replies the mushroom.

"Well, then, the only ones that can walk up into the mangrove swamp are the crabs!"

"You mean those funny, walking crabs are feasting on our fish?" the mushroom asks.

"I think so. Do you know that crabs are the only animals who have their legs on the sides of their bodies instead of under their bodies?"

"Clearly, that has not prevented them from invading our pond," says the mushroom.

"They are probably hiding in the mud right now, ready to feast on our fish!"

"Let's dry out the pond and catch all these crabs! It will make our farmer very happy."

"He will make a lot more money by selling the crabs, and then he will have enough money to pay his kids' school fees."

… and it has only just begun!

The Transformation of Argentina's Economy

Argentinian Map of Opportunities

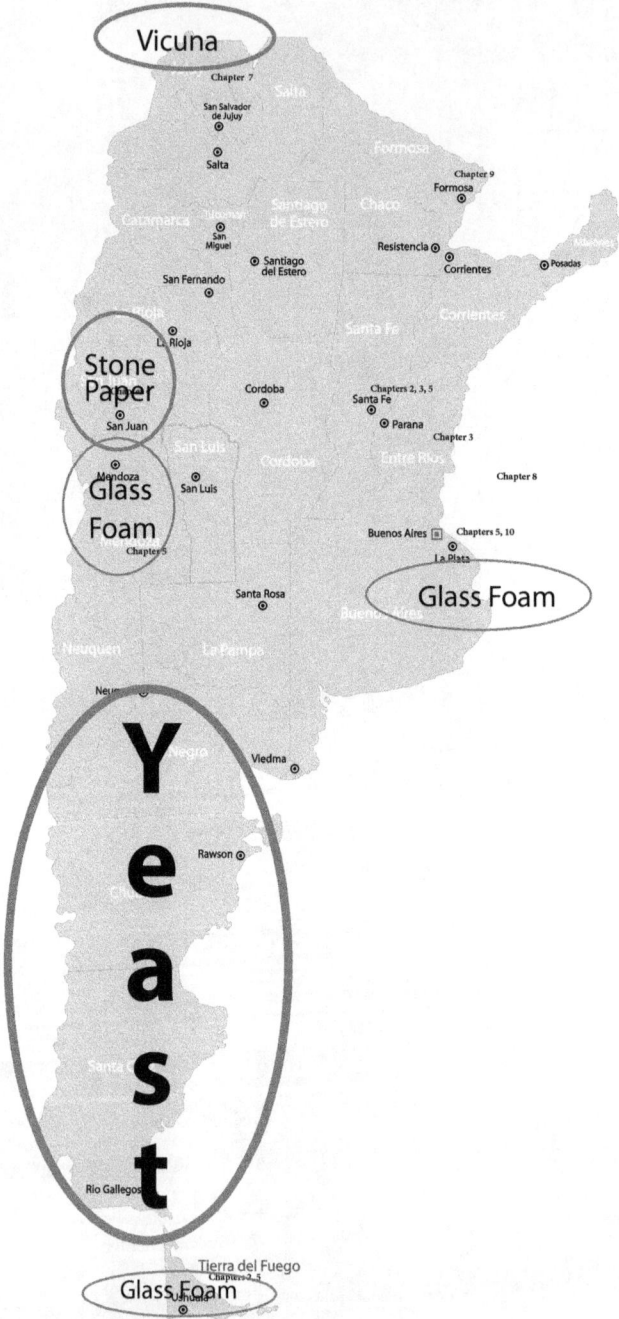

PART B

The Value-Added Game

Plan A

Chapter 4

Saving forests, producing paper from stone

The mobile phone and laptop you use every day may seem rather harmless, merely a practical device, yet that technology is the cause of major pollution and environmental degradation around the world. Modern technology depends on dozens of metals mined from the Earth's crust in a messy process that heavily pollutes the environment and scars the face of the Earth. Mining contaminates the soil and groundwater with dust and chemicals that affect the health of the local population. Mining is also an incredibly inefficient process; for example, gold is purified at an average of two grams per ton, an efficiency of 0.002 percent. This also means that goldmines produce 99.998 percent waste. On average, mines produce 10,000 tons of dust dispersed into the air every year, causing respiratory diseases. This waste also suffocates local vegetation, causes erosion, poisons drinking water, and threatens the health of communities.

Governments aim to control mining pollution with regulation and supervision. As a result, authorities play a game of Hide and Seek with an industry driven by economic motives.

Plan A

Governments are caught in a painful dilemma: mines are an opportunity: they contribute income and employment; mines are also a problem: they cause pollution and threaten public health.

Mines are even a problem for the industry. When the metals can no longer be efficiently retrieved from the earth, the mines are abandoned, and the mining companies must rehabilitate the environment to ensure the mined area is returned close to its original state. This is why mining companies have "closure costs" on their balance sheets. However, even after years of generating good profits, they still don't like it: rehabilitation and closure costs are ongoing sources of conflict and lawsuits

Governments are in urgent need of better mining strategies. The old model does not work: pollution is hardly contained, closing mines are limited to finding trees able to survive on waste dumps, and the remaining ghost towns send communities into downward spirals fed by poverty and violence. Governments need strategies that go beyond the life of the mine as a source of ore and minerals. This is possible if there is a deliberate strategy to turn the polluting waste into an opportunity. They need a strategy that relieves them of the task to act as conflicted policemen who want to prevent harm but are also a part of the problem. Such a strategy exists, and it was invented in China, though the original objective was not to find a way to clean up the mess caused by mining—the tremendous potential of benefits for people and planet was an unexpected side effect, an unintended consequence.

Necessity is the mother of invention. China does not have many trees, nor does it have much water, but the fast-growing country needs paper. It is one of the few countries in the world with a large and continued increase in the consumption of paper. Thus, the Chinese invented stone paper!

This breakthrough innovation was presented in the 1990s by the Lung Meng Technology Group after ten years of research. Lung Meng succeeded in producing paper through mixing crushed stones—calcium carbonate ($CaCO_3$), the most abundant element in the Earth's crust—with high-density polyethylene (HDPE), a standard plastic on the market in desperate search for a method for recycling. Depending on the requirements of the paper, the HDPE content varies from 20 to 40 percent, and it can be recycled indefinitely. It is key that mineral resources, like rocks, and plastics have a useful life—forever. Where could Lung Meng easily and cheaply obtain the raw materials—the rock waste— for this revolutionary new product? In mines— everywhere rock waste from mines lies piled up polluting and changing landscapes.

Stone paper presents the perfect solution for the polluting mines, as waste from mines suddenly has value. Mining companies can sell their burned calcium carbonate for eight dollars per ton, meaning their waste now permits them to make additional money while cleaning up their mess. At the same time, a new stone paper factory nearby can turn that ton of waste into a ton of paper with a value of 1,000 dollars or more, the environment is saved, new income and employment is generated, communities are rebuilt and have a life for decades beyond the closure of the mines. This is the new kind of strategy the mining sector needs worldwide. And it came from an entrepreneur in China, searching for a solution to a completely different problem.

The world market for paper is 400 million tons. The paper market has two main categories: paper used for hygiene products and paper used for printing and packaging. Tissue and toilet paper need to absorb humidity—stone paper could never replace that. However, stone paper does offer a competitive alternative for printing and packaging paper and cartons, an estimated 50 percent of the market, or 200 million tons.

Stone paper has game-changing potential, especially for the packaging industry. The container with milk or fruit juice in your fridge is made from paper—carton, but that functionality requires the paper to resist water and air. This is why, in past decades, composite materials—paper with aluminum or polymer layers—have been developed. Stone paper provides a better solution for packaging materials as it doesn't let air or water through, without the need for any additional layers.

While the overall demand for paper is decreasing around the world—with a few notable exceptions like in China—demand for specialized paper and packaging material is growing. The traditional paper market struggles to supply this demand, despite major efforts to standardize production with the help of chemistry and genetics (GMOs). The industry has concentrated in mega mills producing millions of tons of paper, forcing the closure of smaller, less-efficient production factories. Paper manufacturing is resource-intensive and consumes massive amounts of land, space, and water. Mega mills—like the ones in Uruguay and China—require a complete overhaul of the supply chain infrastructure, including ports, railways, and motorways capable of handling the mega rolls of paper. One ton of paper requires the logging of 20 trees. This means that a five million ton paper production plant devours an amazing 100 million trees per year. As a result, 15 percent of the agricultural land in the world is used to farm trees for paper-making. It's hard to justify maintaining this reliance at a time when there is the growing demand for producing more food.

In this context, sugar cane waste and bamboo offer promising alternative fibers. Growing bamboo for paper production can be 40 times more productive in fiber content per hectare than pine trees over a 50 year period. However, the production of paper from fibers still consumes vast amounts of water, requiring up to 14 liters to produce one A-4 sheet of paper. In a world where millions of people don't have access to clean drinking water, it's hardly acceptable to spill hundreds of billions of liters of water for paper production. The paper industry is meeting this challenge with treatment plants to recycle water, but what about the manufacture of paper from stone which uses no water at all?

Stone paper adds a revolutionary new dimension to the paper market. The paper is made from the waste of mines (coal, gold, copper, etc.) and the processing of the ores. Instead of sacrificing precious agricultural land that can be used to grow food to feed the world while wasting scarce drinking water, stone paper solves an environmental challenge for the mining industry. This is where the nexus of the investment proposal lies. It is through the unlikely combination of the strategic interests of two unrelated industries that a new business opportunity has emerged to change the rules of the game in both.

Lung Meng is currently the only manufacturer in the world,

and it operates four plants in China. Linex in Japan is its only, small, competitor, and it does not export. In the first four years, Lung Meng's production has reached 18,000 tons per year, while the Linex's production in Japan has reached 10,000 tons. The Chinese engineers have recently cracked the challenge of scaling the production system based on extrusion, succeeding in reaching a scale that has changed cost and performance. A total production of one million tons is projected for 2018. Lung Meng is focused on the domestic market but exports stone paper in limited amounts to 50 countries. The company exports 20,000 tons of stone paper to Latin America, a demand growing annually by the double digits. This is where an interesting opportunity for Argentina arises.

Argentina produces 70 percent of the two million tons of paper the country consumes, and it imports the remaining 30 percent, consisting mainly of specialized packaging paper, easily be replaced with locally produced stone paper. In other words, producing stone paper in Argentina would substitute imports, save foreign exchange, and open opportunities for regional export at the same time.

The building of the first stone paper manufacturing plant in Argentina, with an annual capacity of 63,000 tons, would require an investment of 100 million dollars. This comes to about 1,500 dollars per ton, compared to a typical investment cost per ton in a conventional paper mill of 1,500 to 2,000 dollars. The cost per ton of stone paper drops considerably if the capacity of the factory increases to the ideal level of 120,000 tons. Given the low cost of raw materials, a return on investment of 23 percent is projected, based on a pre-feasibility study undertaken with the local governmental and industrial partners. Stone paper offers healthy margins, as lower costs don't need to be translated into lower prices. China shows these projected returns to be realistic. There are no paper mills in the world able to demonstrate a ten-year track record of return on investment in excess of five percent unless they have succeeded in diversifying out of the core business.

The investment in the conversion of mining waste to paper will generate 300 jobs and employment can grow to 1,000 jobs when the factory adds higher-value paper products. The short-term potential for stone paper in Argentina is promising. If the country replaces half of the paper it currently imports with domestic stone paper production, there is a 300,000 ton capacity that could be covered with three more factories.

The first ideal location for a stone paper factory in Argentina is in San Juan province, where 58 percent of the people are employed in the mining industry. Stone paper production would support local development, as value is added to the traditional mining income. Argentina needs economic development in rural areas to prevent further migration to the cities, leading to increasing poverty in vast, non-urban parts of the country. Stone paper manufacturing will also contribute to better public health in San Juan, as the dust the mines produce will be captured for the production of stone paper, rather than trouble the lungs of the local population.

Argentina can become the first pioneer of stone paper in Latin America. Stone paper is a major innovation: it provides a new, ultra-smooth writing experience; it doesn't tear easily; when you drop it in water, the ink remains unchanged, and the paper dries as though it was never wet; it is also fireproof and resists fungi and insects. Unlike natural fibers, no living species thrives on a blend of rock and plastic.

Stone paper has limitations that are gradually being addressed. It takes a bit longer for the ink to dry since there are no fibers to absorb it, so it really has to dry on the surface, meaning rotation presses must run at a slower pace. It can also trigger market innovation to accommodate this new reality. The first generation of stone paper was up to 30 percent heavier than comparable regular paper, increasing distribution costs. This was resolved by the invention of a new generation blending air with the paper during the extrusion process. There's also a challenge with the heat produced by laser printers and copiers, but the trend is toward energy-saving equipment that doesn't need high heat, and therefore, today, nearly all systems are easily able to handle stone paper.

There are, however, vast opportunities for stone paper to replace wood pulp paper. Note that each year, four billion trees are cut for paper production. Chlorine, acid, solvents, and toxic chemicals are required for the whitening of paper made from vegetable fibers. The recycling of cellulose-based paper is also a filthy process, creating wastewater with inks needing special disposal. On the other hand, the ingredient for stone paper— calcium carbonate—is so white by nature, it's already sometimes used as a brightener in the manufacture of ordinary paper.

Stone paper is infinitely recyclable through a new process. Granted, this works best in a business-to-business environment where one does not have to chase the discipline of consumers to dispose of waste paper in the right bin. The used paper is shredded into fine strips, warmed until it has the texture of thick dough, and pressed through pasta-making machines, dried, and broken down into pellets of polyethylene (20 percent) and powder (80 percent), without the need to use chemicals to remove the ink. This is a breakthrough since a minute amount of ink is tolerated in the recycling process. These pellets are extruded for a new batch of paper, without the need for additional plastic in the mix. In other words, plastic is initially required, but it can be reused endlessly to make more paper. This is the first time synthetics are used as they should be, according to their functional capacity—forever. By contrast, paper made from vegetable fibers can be recycled four to six times before the fibers become too short and weak to make a quality product.

Calcium carbonate is cheap and widely available in Argentina. A ton of calcium carbonate has an average value of some eight dollars. Turning the stone into paper increases the value to 1,000 dollars per ton. The value increases to 5,000 dollars per ton with the manufacturing of more than one hundred derivative products, like food packaging cartons, (school) books, notebooks, boxes, bags, etc. A unique opportunity arises to produce cartons used for packaging bananas with stone paper. Latin America ships vast amounts of bananas overseas, the cardboard never returns home and is seldom recycled in the destination countries.

Cardboard cartons have an additional problem: they provide ideal habitats for fungi and insects. Packaging material made from fibers has limitations, from a hygienic perspective. This is why they are covered with polymers. Imagine manufacturing

Plan A

banana cardboards from stone paper. The production of the paper will clean up mine waste in Argentina, and when the boxes reach their destinations in Europe and the United States—the biggest importers of bananas—they can be easily turned into high-quality paper for printing and other uses. And remember: there is no need for water, and no need to plant trees—that's environmental efficiency!

The introduction of stone paper manufacturing will provide governments with a radical new mining strategy that respects the environment while providing new economic development providing communities with long-term opportunities. Stone paper will also make it possible to protect forests and reserve more land for the production of more food. This is the way governments want to do business, turning mining disasters into platforms for new industries attracting investors to generate more income for more people.

The Transformation of Argentina's Economy

Plan A

Clustering mining with paper

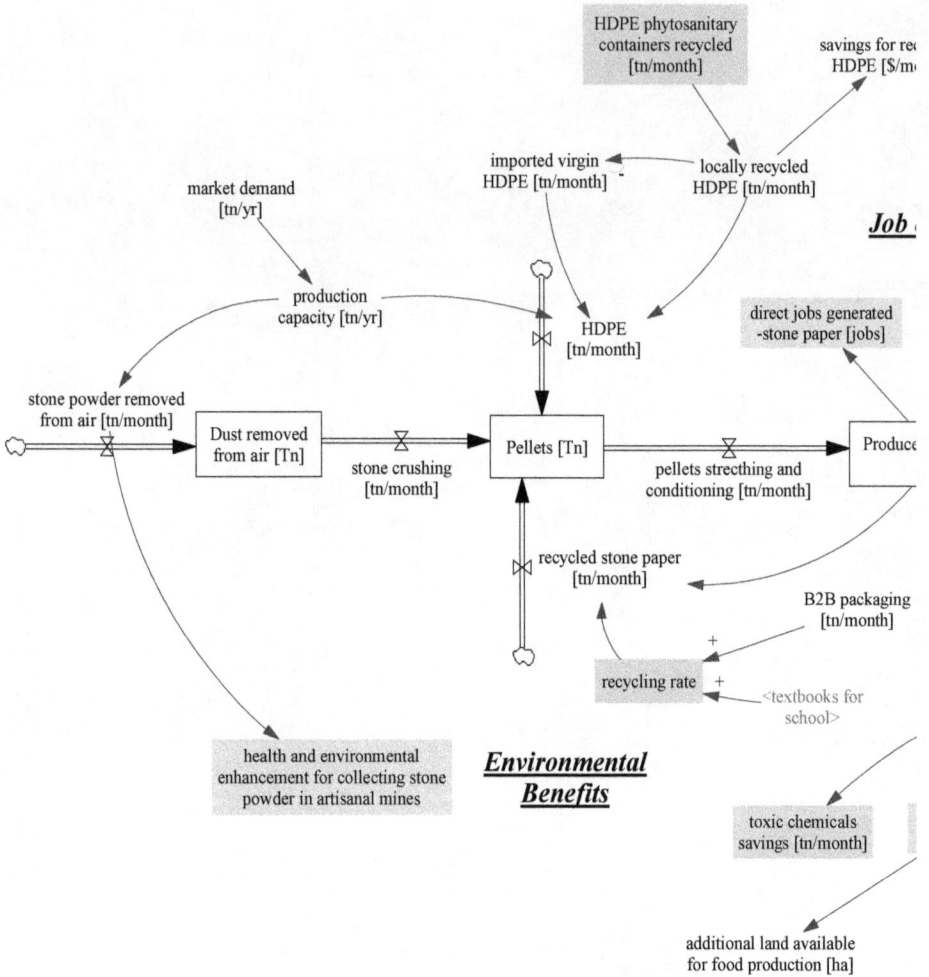

HDPE phytosanitary containers recycled [tn/month]

savings for re‹ HDPE [$/m‹

imported virgin HDPE [tn/month] ⁻

locally recycled HDPE [tn/month]

market demand [tn/yr]

Job ‹

production capacity [tn/yr]

HDPE [tn/month]

direct jobs generated -stone paper [jobs]

stone powder removed from air [tn/month]

Dust removed from air [Tn]

stone crushing [tn/month]

Pellets [Tn]

pellets strecthing and conditioning [tn/month]

Produc‹

recycled stone paper [tn/month]

B2B packaging [tn/month]

recycling rate

<textbooks for school>

health and environmental enhancement for collecting stone powder in artisanal mines

Environmental Benefits

toxic chemicals savings [tn/month]

additional land available for food production [ha]

CO2 produ

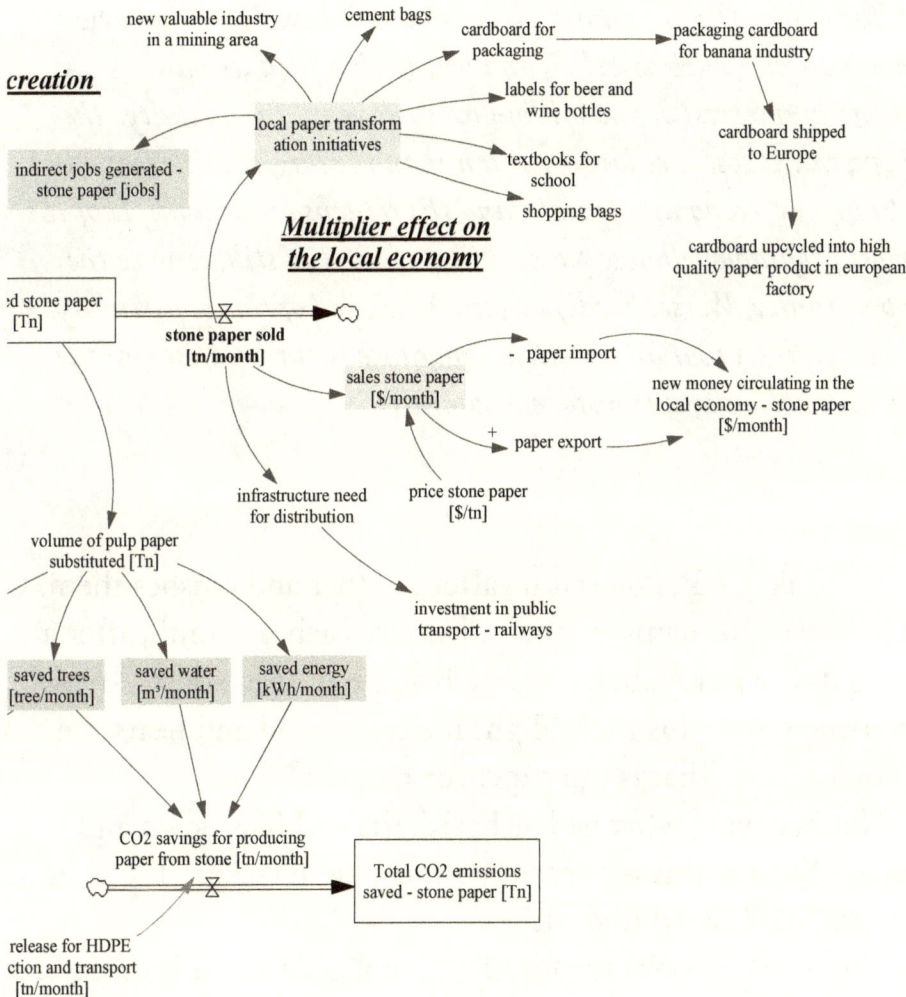

:ycling
onth]

import dependancy
ratio for production

new valuable industry
in a mining area

cement bags

cardboard for
packaging

packaging cardboard
for banana industry

creation

local paper transform
ation initiatives

labels for beer and
wine bottles

cardboard shipped
to Europe

indirect jobs generated -
stone paper [jobs]

textbooks for
school

shopping bags

cardboard upcycled into high
quality paper product in european
factory

*Multiplier effect on
the local economy*

:d stone paper
[Tn]

stone paper sold
[tn/month]

sales stone paper
[$/month]

- paper import

new money circulating in the
local economy - stone paper
[$/month]

+ paper export

infrastructure need
for distribution

price stone paper
[$/tn]

volume of pulp paper
substituted [Tn]

investment in public
transport - railways

saved trees
[tree/month]

saved water
[m³/month]

saved energy
[kWh/month]

CO2 savings for producing
paper from stone [tn/month]

Total CO2 emissions
saved - stone paper [Tn]

release for HDPE
ction and transport
[tn/month]

Fable 5

Stone paper

The first reaction to stone paper is incredulity. This innovation has been met with disbelief, and yet, with a production capacity in excess of one million tons per year, it is a reality. The investment costs are lower per ton than the largest mills searching the highest economies of scale, and the returns are a multiple of the most profitable cellulose paper mills today. And still, few see the opportunity. Worse, hardly anyone has heard of this opportunity. This confirms that all too often, ignorance is our greatest obstacle to innovation and transformation.

A monkey takes one stone after another and crushes them. He swings his hammer and pulverizes each one until, after a long day of hard labor, he has a big pile of stone dust. An owl starting out on his night flight hovers around and hears the monkey say, "That is the paper for the day."

Not believing what he has heard, the owl flies down and asks, "You say this is paper? You must be mistaken. These are stones, hammered to dust."

The monkey looks surprised and replies, "Oh, so, how do you make paper?"

"Well," says the owl, "our paper is made from fiber. There are many fibers available, from fast-growing trees, for instance, but the problem is they are taking all of the food from the soil, and they drink too much water".

"So, what is your solution?"

"We are working with bamboo. You know it grows quickly, as it is a grass. You cut it, and it grows again."

"And do you need any water to turn bamboo into paper?"

"Of course. Making paper requires water—a lot of water. The good news is that bamboo comes with its own water."

"That's great. My stone paper, however, does not need any water at all."

"That can't be true! You may fool many people, but I tell you: paper is made from fiber and needs water."

"Well, it is time to think outside of the box, you supposedly 'wise' owl."

"That is not very respectful, my young friend. Never in my life have I seen a single sheet of paper made without fiber."

"And never in my life have I come across such a stubborn monkey."

"Hey, could you show a bit more respect for an old owl like me?"

"Of course. If you could be open to new ideas that have already been put into practice! By mixing stone dust with recycled plastic bottles and some chalk, I can make paper for writing and packaging without cutting any trees down or wasting a drop of water."

"Paper that is tree-free and water-free?" wonders the owl.

"Exactly! This paper can also be recycled forever and ever, and all of the land used to grow trees can now be used to grow food. It will also create many jobs from bits of rock and stone which are waste products."

Plan A

"More farms and more fields growing food? I like that. It means more mice for me!" says the owl with a smile.

...and it has only just begun!

Chapter 5

Turning trash into cash: the transformation of glass

The recycling of glass along with paper is arguably one of the most successful waste recovery programs in the world. About one-third of all glass produced in the United States is recycled; the European Union, on average, recycles three-quarters of its used glass; and Switzerland leads the world with a glass recycling rate of 98 percent. Countries like Argentina have yet to start a recycling program with any impact—most of its used glass ends up in landfills or dumps—and It may see the European recycling successes as distant dreams.

However, the recycling of glass is not a big success. Rather, it is a missed opportunity and has been for decades, and Argentina has a chance to do something much more useful and lucrative with used glass. Here's the critical point: it does not make sense to crush a perfect glass bottle to make a new glass bottle. It is very costly to melt glass and create the same thing with the same value. From an environmental perspective, this can never be a profitable business.

This is why the time has come to make a shift from recycling as a way to merely deal with waste and decrease the load on landfills to an investment strategy based on generating new value. Nature never recycles a product into the same product. No tree tries to recycle its leaves, keeping the foliage from the autumn to be re-attached in the spring. Instead, a tree drops its leaves, which are converted through armies of species— including earthworms, ants, fungi, and micro-organisms—into humus, which feeds the tree again through the roots, blended with rain and bird poop. Every element contributes to this never-ending process.

This is a remarkable lesson in industrial ecology. Just like it does not make sense for a tree to recycle its leaves, it does not make sense to turn glass bottles into glass bottles. The tree passes through the humus stage before the nutrients are transformed into leaves again. Similarly, glass bottles are better converted into another material of greater use to others on the market. We propose foam glass. Converting used glass into foam glass means turning waste into a structural material for the building industry, as well as into a range of other, useful products that add a new and higher value for agriculture and furniture manufacturing. Foam glass provides a compelling example as to how one product, by its design and systemic use, can eliminate the need for several products. This creates a new dimension for sustainability, as well as economic development.

Construction is, remarkably enough, from an environmental perspective, the most destructive activity on the planet. To build something new and beautiful, we first create a lot of damage and waste. The construction sector is a painful example of resource inefficiency, responsible for at least 50 percent of the total annual consumption of natural resources. The sector uses 40 percent of the energy consumed in the world, producing between 40 and 50 percent of the total waste. The ecological footprint of building is immense. Every square meter of a new building requires two tons of raw materials, and a lot of water and energy is needed to extract these resources. The energy necessary to build a house represents a third of the annual energy consumption of the family that will live in the home over the next 50 years!

In other words, there's an urgent need for new models and new processes to reduce waste and environmental impact in the construction sector while making better use of locally available resources. Foam glass presents an attractive, sustainable alternative technology to building new housing with high energy efficiency, exceptional health conditions, and environmental quality.

Foam glass is not a new innovation. Invented in the 1930s, Pittsburgh Corning in the United States has been producing the material for decades in large volumes. This massive production scale would not serve Argentina well as production efficiencies would be lost, given the high distribution costs related to shipping heavy glass through a vast country. However, the technology is becoming increasingly relevant in a world looking for better, environmental performance. Foam glass also allows for much smaller-scale local production based on cheaply and readily available raw materials. The production of foam glass would clean up waste, and there's no need to extract anything from nature. Foam glass fulfills multiple functions, thus offering multiple services in a single product. This makes it possible to vastly increase material efficiency, which is exactly what is needed to improve both ecological footprint and return on capital.

Plan A

Foam glass is made by crushing glass—used bottles and window glass from the auto and construction industries, diverted from landfills or collected from recycling points—into a "glass flour" that is subsequently heated and blended, at melting point, with CO_2 gas, creating a bubbly foam. This means that foam glass production captures CO_2 and contributes to the fight against global warming, in a process that does not require water. After cooling, the mixture hardens into rigid, porous blocks with gas-filled, closed-cell pores, comprising 97 percent of its volume. Foam glass is very light, but it is also very strong, which makes it a superior construction material. Because of the "trapped gas," the thermal and acoustic insulating capacity of foam glass is 20 percent higher than other insulating materials. Glass doesn't catch fire; it only melts at 1,100°C. Consequently, foam glass acts as a flame-retardant, as well. Glass is inert, making the proliferation of bacteria and fungus impossible, so this saves on the chemicals to keep a room free of bugs while reducing the risk for respiratory diseases.

The opportunity for a sustainable housing industry emerges with wooden or metal house frames "filled" with foam glass blocks made of reconditioned glass from bottles and windshields. Koljern, a Swedish company, has pioneered prefabricated housing systems based on foam glass. The excellent insulating capacity of foam glass makes the material especially fitting for colder or warmer climates. It also means that additional materials for insulation are unnecessary, which generates savings because there is no need for toxic flame retardants in the house construction. Foam glass also provides excellent pest-control qualities, and no molds will grow on it. Finally, the material has a durability of around 100 years, and can be 100 percent recycled after that. Glass can always be recycled and reconditioned, and it loses neither value nor functionality. In fact, it should be viewed as an asset on a balance sheet, not as a cost on a profit and loss statement.

Foam glass offers more opportunities beyond construction material. It can be used as a growth medium for tomatoes and strawberries in greenhouses and hydroponic systems, as the porous structure of foam glass offers soil aeration and the right water balance for the roots. Earthstone, an American company, has been manufacturing cleaning products from foam glass for 25 years. The abrasive, "pumice-like" structure of foam glass allows for the cleaning of kitchen and bathroom sinks, toilets, and grills without the need for toxic chemicals or sanding products. Earthstone products help reduce the strip-mining of pumice and other minerals used in many commercial abrasive products.

So far, Europe leads the foam glass market. In the past decade, 11 factories have been built—four of which are operated by Misapor AG in "glass-recycling-champion," Switzerland. The Swiss even have an investment fund dedicated solely to this activity. Calculations show that a commercial factory can be sustainable and profitable with an annual intake of 5.2 million glass bottles. To get a sense of the potential of this new industry, the French and Americans are the biggest wine drinkers in the world, consuming about four billion bottles of wine every year. This means there is an opportunity to build some 750 glass recycling factories in both countries. Argentineans drink some 1.25 billion bottles of wine annually. This glass—which includes neither bottles or recycled glass from the car and construction industries—is enough to successfully operate almost 250 factories in the country!

In reality, foam glass factories will be clustered around population centers. This is so the waste glass can be easily collected. A foam glass factory requires a population of about 50,000 people, an investment of 15 million dollars, and can be built in about 18 months. The return on investment is estimated between 15 and 20 percent. It is important to note that a foam glass factory can produce various products, from building blocks for the construction industry to cleaning products for consumers. This means that risks can be spread. One factory can employ about 25 people. Indirectly, at least two to three times as many new jobs will be generated for the collection of used glass in the construction industry and the establishment of new industries, like pre-fabricated housing, and hydroponic food production. The raw material for foam glass offers a new platform for entrepreneurship that will generate employment beyond what the traditional glass industry has to offer.

Foam glass will offer Argentina the opportunity to develop a prefabricated housing industry. Pre-fabrication will allow for interesting efficiencies. The material is especially relevant in the area of Buenos Aires. Argentina's capital is located at the confluence of three rivers. Many people live on small islands in the vast river estuaries. Inundations happen frequently, and consequently, humidity is an ongoing challenge in the local housing sector. Concrete foundations are prone to mold, affecting living conditions and population health. Foam glass foundations can solve that humidity problem. This makes Buenos Aires the perfect target for foam glass factories. Not only is there plenty of glass waste available, but the conditions in the construction market are also ideal for the introduction of this product innovation.

Tierra del Fuego in the deep south of the country also provides a great opportunity for foam glass. Not only has the local government recently introduced a glass recycling program, but Tierra del Fuego's distance from Argentina's heartland makes local construction material production a very good investment. Today, construction materials need to travel 3,000 kilometers from Buenos Aires. The local government has concluded that shipping the collected, used glass to a recycling facility is too expensive. Building a foam glass factory will solve both problems at the same time: the collected glass can be locally reconditioned, and the need to ship building materials to Tierra del Fuego from far away will substantially decrease.

Another opportunity arises in the wine country around Mendoza. This city has a population of 115,000 people, the perfect size for a foam glass factory. However, Mendoza's winemakers produce some 150 million wine bottles per year and one percent—or 1.5 million bottles—is usually discarded due to production errors; this waste is the perfect raw material for use in a foam glass factory.

Furthermore, Argentina will benefit from this new industry because locally produced foam glass will replace the import of insulation materials. The production of foam glass is the perfect example of an opportunity to turn trash into cash. Today, used glass ends up in landfills. This "waste" can be used to create healthier living environments, as well as healthier cleaning products for consumers.

Glass is a resource, and it is timely that Cerveza Quilmes, Argentina's leading brewery, recently reconfirmed its decision to only bottle beer in glass, skipping the world trend of aluminum packaging. The brewery did not realize this decision meant supporting the country's housing sector! This is the new economy, where systems of industries support each other.

In an old-fashioned, life-cycle analysis, glass loses from plastic. Glass is heavier, which leads to higher distribution costs. The soft drink company only sees the bottle, and the opportunity to cut expenses by choosing a lighter container needing no subsequent handling. This decision pushes the waste into society, while communities lose the opportunity to generate value, income, and employment.

In a wider systems approach, glass beats plastic by handsomely—even if it is biodegradable—in any lifecycle analysis. Foam glass reduces the use of natural resources and energy. Every ton of foam glass saves a ton of resources through mining. Glass is mined from sand once, and it can be used—and add value—forever.

This is a different kind of sustainability, focused not just on the impact on the environment, but on people, as well. A home provides more than a roof. Housing is even more sustainable when it supports the health of people. Healthier living supports better opportunities for education and employment. The inspiring message is that one, simple decision to value glass will have a deep, positive impact on many parts of society.

Plan A

Clustering packaging with construction

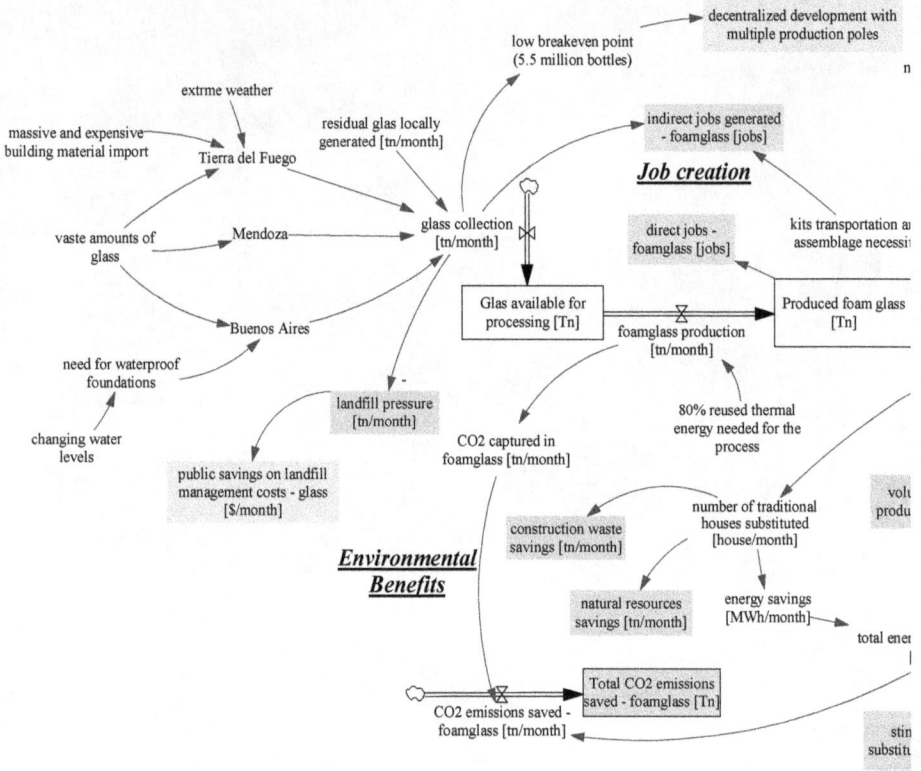

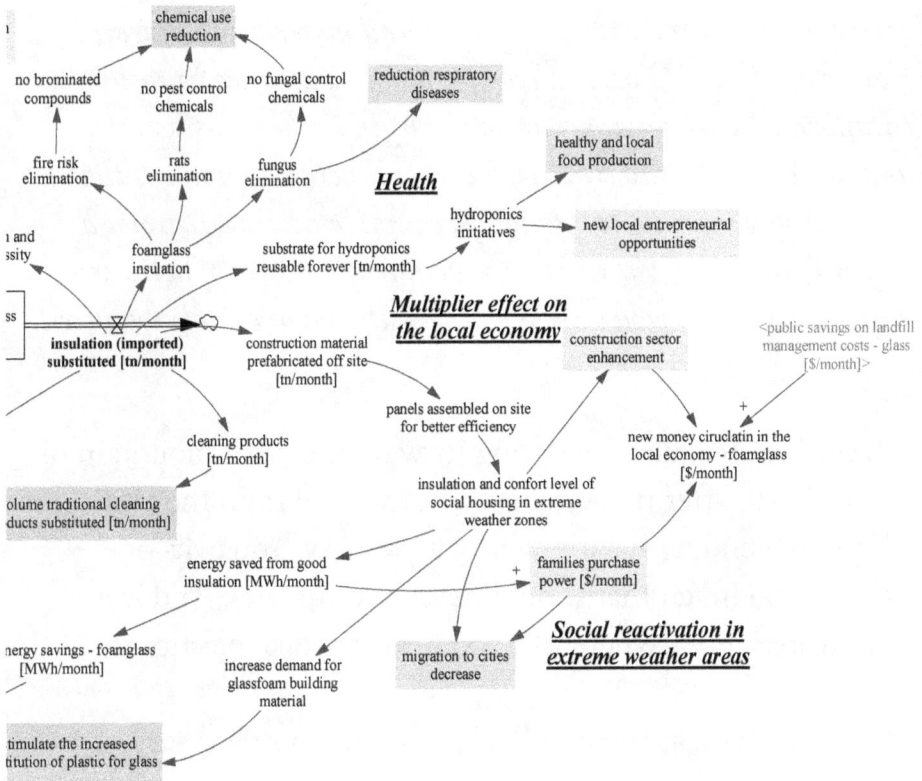

chemical use reduction

no brominated compounds

no pest control chemicals

no fungal control chemicals

reduction respiratory diseases

fire risk elimination

rats elimination

fungus elimination

Health

healthy and local food production

hydroponics initiatives

new local entrepreneurial opportunities

foamglass insulation

substrate for hydroponics reusable forever [tn/month]

Multiplier effect on the local economy

insulation (imported) substituted [tn/month]

construction material prefabricated off site [tn/month]

construction sector enhancement

<public savings on landfill management costs - glass [$/month]>

panels assembled on site for better efficiency

cleaning products [tn/month]

new money ciruclatin in the local economy - foamglass [$/month]

insulation and confort level of social housing in extreme weather zones

olume traditional cleaning ducts substituted [tn/month]

energy saved from good insulation [MWh/month]

families purchase power [$/month]

nergy savings - foamglass [MWh/month]

increase demand for glassfoam building material

migration to cities decrease

Social reactivation in extreme weather areas

timulate the increased titution of plastic for glass

The crystal palace

The key to the transformation of an economy is the identification of new value in and around products and materials that are readily available. Glass is already separated, and can be easily transformed with great profit and margin for business, society, and nature—not into a bottle, but into functional products that dramatically increase the economy's overall efficiency. It is not a recycling program, but rather, the design of a cluster of activities responding to everyone's needs with cheap and available resources.

A flock of seagulls is working its way through a mountain of waste. Truck after truck delivers more waste from the city.

"It is astounding what people throw away," squawks one. "There is so much that should never end up here. And it is even worse at sea, where fish and birds mistake plastics for food."

"Yes, just look at these millions of plastic bottles," says another.

"I don't understand how people could ever have been fooled into believing that plastic is better than glass," adds a rat who lives in the same area.

"You never went to school—I can tell," answers the first seagull. "I learned there that plastic is light and glass is heavy so that you can carry more in a plastic bottle."

"But what can you do with the bottles lying around here?"

wonders the rat.

"You could make new bottles." The young seagull puffs out his feathers, happy with his answer.

"Have you ever seen leaves drop from a tree in autumn?" asks the rat.

"Of course. Again, this is something you do not need to go to school in order to understand," scoffs the seagull.

"But have you ever seen a tree reattaching the leaves it dropped way back in autumn come springtime?"

"Now, don't be ridiculous. We know that does not work, and if it ever were to work, it would cost a lot, be inefficient, and would never look as good."

"So, if the tree does not make leaves out of leaves, why do you want to make bottles out of bottles?"

"Umm…because I was told so," confesses the seagull.

"You believe everything they tell you? Let's put our heads together. Let's do better," says the rat.

"Sure, I'll give it a try," promises the seagull.

"What happens if the glass melts? What happens if the plastic melts?"

"Well, plastic burns, creating black smoke that smells terrible. Even worse, it is bad for you and me."

"And glass?"

"Glass just melts, and if there is a lot of gas around—which we do have—then it turns into foam."

"And what do you do with foam glass?"

"I have no idea!"

"Think again—is it heavy?" asks the rat.

"No."

"Can you bite into it?"

"I don't want to. Can you?"

"No—if I try, I might lose my teeth," answers the rat. "Does it allow water through?" he continues.

"No."

"Can you sit on it?"

"Yes. It is strong!" The seagull nods, happy to know the answer.

"And if you crush it to pieces, what can you do with it?"

"Well, glass cannot be destroyed, only transformed," answers the seagull.

"It looks like we could build a house out of this!" exclaims the rat.

"Well, now, I have to go back to school and teach everyone to use much more glass so we can have our crystal palace!"

... And it only has just begun!

Chapter 6

A wealth of yeast in Patagonia

The vast and sparsely populated plains of Patagonia, shared by Argentina and Chile, offer an abundance of nature. The region comprises the southern section of the Andes Mountains and stretches from the Pacific Ocean in the west to the Atlantic Ocean in the east. Situated between high mountains and two oceans, Patagonia offers a wealth of biodiversity. Many visitors marvel at Patagonia's expansive beauty. They see the lush animals, shiny birds, surprising insects, and wealth of plants, yet there is so much remaining unseen to the human eye.

Few people are aware that Patagonia, jointly with the Himalayas, offers the richest variety of tiny organisms playing a critical role in our lives: yeast.

Without yeast, our lives would not be the same—we would have no bread, no sanitation, no conservation, and no fermentation, meaning there would be no beer, wine, kimchi, or tofu. The thousands of yeasts that thrive in Patagonia offer Argentina a unique opportunity to generate economic development with a resource that is readily available for free.

Yeasts are single-celled, micro-organisms classified,

along with molds and mushrooms, as members of the fungi kingdom. They are (almost) invisible, and hang out in trees with ripening fruit and on the bark of oaks. Early civilizations discovered that yeasts triggered fermentation, that is, converting carbohydrates into carbon dioxide and alcohol. The process of fermentation sanitized food and cleansed water. Today, we may associate beer with alcohol, but the original use of beer was as an alternative for water carrying disease and germs. The ancient Egyptians used yeast fermentation to leaven bread, which dramatically increased digestion. Yeast has also long been used to ferment grapes into wine.

There are over 1,500 species of yeast known to scientists and many more that have not been studied yet. When the season is right, traditional beer brewers in Belgium open the roof to "harvest" the yeast used for fermentation. British company Cara Technology offers the food and beverage industry some 800 varieties of yeast it has collected in the world. However, today, most yeast is produced in labs in standardized, genetically modified processes ensuring predictable flavors and tastes. Society has mostly lost the richness of yeast diversity and the wealth of flavors and experiences they can produce.

More and more, people are looking beyond standard products to exclusive experiences. Yes, beer multinationals control most of the market, but in every city, micro-breweries offer a beer-drinking experience that is not standard but local and unique. There are 1,000 micro-breweries in Argentina and counting. There is a large wine culture in the country, as well, and a vast majority of the yeast for these drinks is imported, while

Argentina possesses the world's largest reserve of yeasts with over 1,000 varieties in Patagonia!

Argentina has a major opportunity to become the world's number one supplier of yeasts to create diverse and unique flavors in wine, beer, bread, and more, across the globe. To illustrate the emerging trend, in collaboration with scientific network COCINET, Heineken recently launched a new, exclusive, limited edition beer that—according to the label—is fermented with Patagonian wild yeast. This initiative shows that the know-how to use yeast varieties for large-scale production is available. The next step is the establishment of a network of citizens, biologists, scholars, students, and nature lovers who will work in collaboration with local laboratories to harvest the yeasts. This network will be the basis for the development of inventory build-up, with the exact location of where in nature the yeast was found and will lead to a distribution and export program to enrich the dynamic micro and craft brewing industry. It is an industry that already has more than 100,000 operations worldwide (65,000 in the US alone) with native yeast species from the Patagonian wild that can even be traced to specific areas.

Science makes it possible to identify yeast sources with great precision. This means it is possible to prevent "bio-piracy" by commercial companies who have taken the liberty to collect endemic yeast species under the cover of science. These companies "steal" yeasts and make money selling it without retribution or recognition to the ecosystems hosting these unique, living organisms.

Decades ago, Esprit-founder, Douglas Tompkins, and

his wife, Kris, began to buy vast areas of land in Chile and Argentina to restore the environment and return it to the governments as national parks for future generations. Today, the development of a micro yeast industry makes it possible to create an income stream to maintain that precious nature. This also provides the opportunity to bring science and entrepreneurship together to preserve the last tracts of primary rainforests. The re-emerging story of yeast offers many other experiences, as well. It provides opportunities to re-connect children with nature and educate them about food and how to create resilience by making their own food. Bread, beer, and wine are in every home of every Argentinian. This is a way to bring biodiversity and the economic value of preservation of the ecosystems to every Argentinean. "Yeast safaris" can be a new offering in ecotourism in which tourists would go out into nature to map and catalog yeasts, bringing art and science together. "With yeast from Patagonia" could become a new "trademark," strengthening the Argentinian "brand" across the world. And a two percent wilderness tax on all beer, bread, and wine produced with wild yeast from Patagonia could generate a massive revenue stream to conserve threatened primary ecosystems.

Patagonian yeasts can offer an innovative economic model. National parks featuring on the list of expenses for the government's common good can become a source of substantial revenue. Wild yeasts sell for 25 dollars a kilo. There already exists a ready market of beer brewers and winemakers that can be supplied and which is very keen to buy. The artisanal beer industry has been growing at an annual rate of

40 percent for a while, with no signs of deceleration. After years of industry consolidation, there is a clear trend toward local- and small-scale production, with a wealth in creative beer design.

As a first step, Argentina has decided to invest in a laboratory to study yeasts and to provide education and training to breweries, winemakers, and people in the food industry. It has experts like Dr. Diego Libkind who created the first yeast maps and even discovered the ancient mother cultures of European lager beers, tracing them back to Patagonia. There is a remarkable story to be told, and there are millions prepared to listen and buy.

It is a small investment to create more awareness to will support the opening of a vast new market, valued at one billion dollars a year. The experts agree: the Andes Mountain Range has the right image to turn this into a strong business case. The collection can be based on thousands of entrepreneurs; the purification can be based on dozens of local production units; and Patagonia's brand and name recognition are already solid in the world. It is up to investors to turn this into a competitive industry. In its (still) abundant ecosystem, Patagonia will continue to produce yeasts for free. The opportunity for Argentina is to offer this variety to the world to inspire diverse flavors and generate new income and economic development, while saving money on imports and generating a stable revenue for the national parks with products common to every household, worldwide. It will energize a new generation and instill a respect for nature, thanks to the small and invisible biodiversity.

Plan A

Clustering Yeast with beer, bread and wine

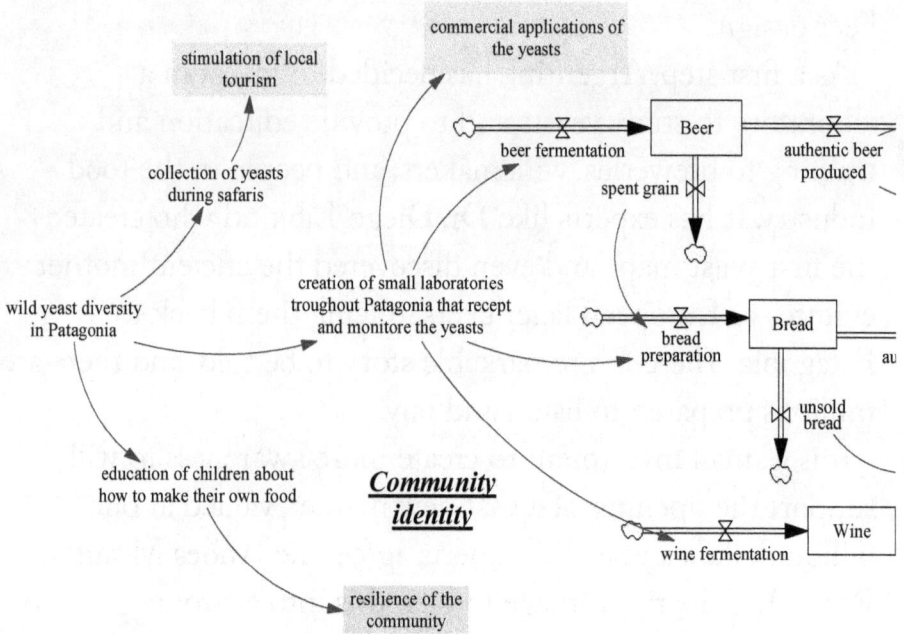

stimulation of local tourism

commercial applications of the yeasts

collection of yeasts during safaris

beer fermentation

Beer

authentic beer produced

spent grain

creation of small laboratories troughout Patagonia that recept and monitore the yeasts

wild yeast diversity in Patagonia

bread preparation

Bread

au

unsold bread

education of children about how to make their own food

Community identity

resilience of the community

wine fermentation

Wine

The Transformation of Argentina's Economy

Multiplier effect in the local economy

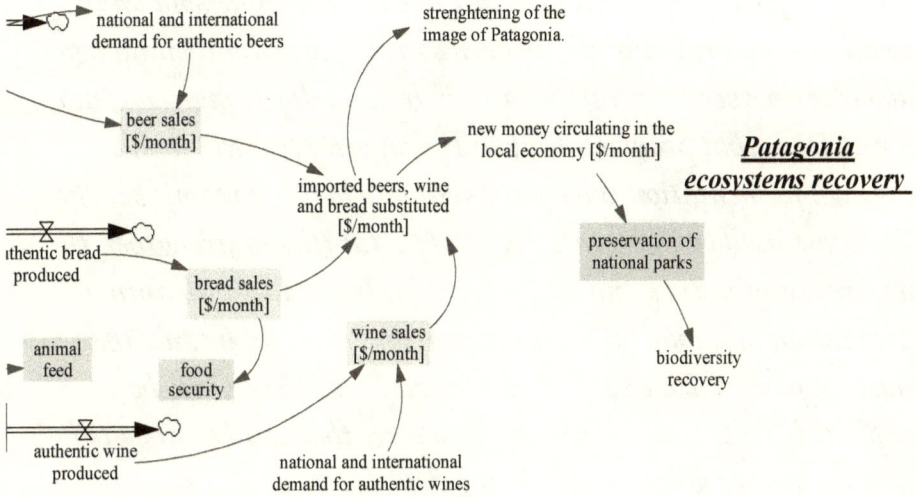

national and international demand for authentic beers

strenghtening of the image of Patagonia.

beer sales [$/month]

new money circulating in the local economy [$/month]

Patagonia ecosystems recovery

imported beers, wine and bread substituted [$/month]

ithentic bread produced

preservation of national parks

bread sales [$/month]

animal feed

wine sales [$/month]

food security

biodiversity recovery

authentic wine produced

national and international demand for authentic wines

Fable 7

Small but powerful

Yeast is part of everyday life. Just like ecosystems depend on the small and nearly invisible, modern society learned millennia ago about the power to transform a raw, hard to digest material into a nutrition that promotes health. The capacity to create value through fermentation with yeast will also bring economic benefits. The yeast itself can generate major opportunities to strengthen the awareness of nature and its biodiversity beyond its lush animal population and colorful plants to generate jobs and finance the natural parks with endogenous resources that have yet to be exploited. Yeast is one of the only resources that can be harvested and multiplied without ever being depleted, provided the ecosystem remains thriving.

A small owl is watching the rainfall in a beautiful, Patagonian valley. The forest is wet, but the smell is fresh. There is something special in the air.

The owl spots a mara hopping around the bush. "Are you a rabbit or a kangaroo?" wonders the owl.

"What continent do you call home?" responds the mara.

"This is Patagonia, the land of space, plenty, and beauty."

"Well, in that case. I cannot be a kangaroo," snips the mara.

"Maybe you are not, but you hop around like one."

"Look, I am a mara. I may look like a rabbit and hop around like a kangaroo, but just forget both. I am original, and natural, and I'm called a mara."

"Sorry, but I've hardly ever seen you. There must be only a few of you around. What happened to the rest of the family?"

"Killed!"

"Oh, I am so sorry."

"Don't feel sorry for me. I feel sorry for you. You must be a dwarf owl. Did you parents not feed you?"

"People call me a pygmy owl, I'm a teeny-weenie bird destined to look like a miniature version of my big brothers, but I have a big tail."

"And what do you eat?"

"Mice, lizards, small birds, and occasionally an earthworm."

"We both live in a wonderful world called Patagonia."

"Not only do we love to live in this world, but we share this world with some wonderful friends."

"Who is your best friend?"

"Maybe they aren't my best friends, but they're my smallest and most powerful friends: I adore all yeasts in this forest."

"Yeast? You have got to be kidding! That tiny invisible stuff that hangs around ripening fruit and nestles on tree bark? It can even make people sick."

"I admire the stuff that's too small for the human eye to see and what makes our beer, wine, and bread so tasty."

"You really have no better choice to put on a pedestal?"

"It's so small yet so powerful. Wild yeast turns juice into wine, barley into beer, and dough into bread. We can go and catch it on a yeast safari."

"Wow, it is about time I figured out something great I can do for this world."

Plan A

"Why don't you figure out what you can do with yeasts? There are thousands of them around, and each one of them can do the magic for you!"

... *And it only has just begun!*

Chapter 7

The Wild Fibers

The clothes we wear are either made from farmed fibers—cotton and wool, or synthetic fibers—nylon and many others. This textiles market is dominated by a few big players that are able to operate within very small margins, but thanks to their enormous volume, generate huge profits. In this stressful environment, smaller players like Argentina—despite their historical market presence and the millions of sheep in Patagonia—can't successfully compete. Argentina, however, has an opportunity to make a unique contribution to the high-fashion market while serving its indigenous cultures and communities. The country has access to wild fibers of exceptional quality that can be obtained by rebuilding traditions that have been thriving in the Andes for nearly ten millennia. Wild fibers offer a very high margin, and the emerging industry maintains and regenerates fragile ecosystems. It seems too good to be true, but field visits and detailed follow-ups with the communities have offered insight enough into these opportunities to transform business models for generations to come. This is not a hit and run opportunity—rather, it requires care and design with a lasting impact.

Plan A

A high market concentration opens opportunities for high-quality, niche players that can offer a higher value with respect for tradition and culture. We can draw a parallel between the textiles business and the drink industry. Most beer in the world is produced and sold by a handful multi-national breweries, however, there's an inspiring trend of micro-breweries and/or cafes that emerge in every modern city. Similarly, there are a few giant textile players, and now there's an opportunity in the global market for products that add local flavors and styles at a premium price. Top brands and designers are looking for different fabrics to create exclusive fashions, and in their search, they have come to the highlands of Argentina where, for 10,000 years, a not so well-known animal, the vicuña has lived in symbiosis with local mountain communities. Today, vicuña wool is the most sought-after in the world. The vicuña offers Argentina a unique economic, social, and environmental opportunity, provided it changes the business model of the export of raw materials and strengthens the communities to rediscover their skills and affinity with the fiber, the vicuña, and its ecosystem.

A century ago, the world textiles market consisted only of farmed natural fibers of mostly wool and cotton. The invention of nylon in the 1930s was the beginning of a major market transformation. Gradually, natural fibers lost their market share, as the new synthetic fibers were easier and cheaper to produce, wash, and dry. Today, synthetic fibers hold almost 65 percent of the world market. Natural fibers share the remaining 35 percent, with cotton holding the lion's share with 25 percent. Wool has a marginal one percent of the world market. One hundred years ago, one million tons of silk were sold each year; today the world silk market is less than 100,000 tons.

Over the past ten years, the market has undergone another transformation, with fashion becoming increasingly dominated by cheaply- and quickly-produced cotton clothing that is only briefly used until the next fashion wave hits. This trend is led by global brands, such as Inditex (Spain), Hennes & Mauritz (Sweden), and Bestseller (Denmark).

"Fast fashion" dramatically increases the environmental and social burdens caused by the fiber industry. The production of both synthetic and natural fibers poses a huge environmental challenge due to the massive amounts of water used in the process. The conversion of each kilogram of cotton seeds into fiber, for example, requires a staggering 2,000 liters of water. Moreover, cotton is highly dependent on chemicals. According to some estimates, cotton is responsible for as much as 20 percent of the pesticides applied to crops worldwide. In other words, cotton production drains water resources, polluting water systems with toxins at the same time. Organic cotton removes the toxins from production, but the water consumption, the color pigments, and the fixing agents remain problematic. It's not surprising that the United States of America, once the largest producer of cotton, has resolutely decided to reduce its farming of the material because it simply no longer has the water to continue.

The aggressive drive by global fashion brands to lower prices has not only concentrated cotton production, but it has also forced production countries to undercut (child) labor standards. China and India lead the market, together producing 60 percent of the world's cotton. Smaller players—like Indonesia, Bangladesh, and Pakistan—are able to maintain a market position. Other countries—like Argentina—struggle to successfully compete under the stressful circumstance of ever lower unit prices for ever lower quality products.

Alternatively, the production of synthetic fibers requires large-scale investments related to the fossil fuel industry, as well as easy access to large consumer markets. Argentina does not seem to be well-positioned for that industry, either.

Finally, there is the wool market. The sheep of Patagonia—introduced by Spanish colonizers—provide some four percent of the world's wool production of two million tons, but wool is not very popular in today's fashion industry, and few sheep farms do well. Sheep's wool sells for about three dollars per kilo, which leaves minimal margin for the herder. Economies of scale do not seem to add to the overall position of wool in the world market, even though niche players, like the Norwegians, succeed in maintaining their wool with great national pride, supported by a local market ready to pay extraordinary premium prices, and a government ready to generously subsidize.

The general conclusion is that producing fibers for the textile industry doesn't offer production countries interesting opportunities to add value to support local economic development. The oversimpLiFied approach to production in ever-higher volumes has led to a situation where cost-cutting and budget controls determine everything. Operations are focused on offering ever-cheaper products with ever-better margins for the intermediaries, without considering the full impact on the health and the lives of people and their environment.

As an example, if you wear a fine, soft, cashmere sweater, you are likely contributing to the desertification of Mongolia. The country produces 40 percent of all cashmere through herding goats in the fringes of the savannas around the Gobi Desert, but cashmere production doesn't help Mongolia. When you buy a cashmere sweater online, PayPal—a financial software system—earns as much on the sale for securing the payment as the herder does for accompanying his animals all year.

The only way for herders to survive in these circumstances of rising demand and limited space is to cut costs where they can, or so they are made to believe. The simplest way to increase revenues is by owning as many goats as possible. This will bring the overhead expenses for washing, spinning, dying, weaving, sewing, and selling the wool down. So, the greater the number of grazing goats in Mongolia's fragile savanna bordering dry lands, the more the desert expands. There is a direct correlation between the herders' livelihood and the degradation of the ecosystem. More goats may temporarily increase the herders' income, but the fashion chains will keep pushing the prices down to meet the higher consumer demand and desertification will continue; it is a predictable recipe for disaster.

Nature can only be maintained and regenerated after the herders' livelihood is secured. This means substantially raising the price the herders receive for cashmere. Experiments have shown that Mongolian herders can substantially increase their income with the introduction of a model of vertical integration from wool to wear. In this new experimental model, the farmer gets ten percent of the price paid by the customer for a sweater. The farmer directly participates in the success and the quality of the product. Such a model transforms the production from delivering a commodity to creating products with a high value. The new model allows herders in Mongolia to generate greater income with fewer goats. This takes pressure off the environment and permits nature to restore itself.

Vertical integration may not seem efficient according to the doctrine of standardization, but it does permit differentiation. It also increases opportunities for local artisans to add creativity and cultural dimensions to produce desirable fabrics and clothing. A fully integrated value chain offers a broad opportunity for craftspeople to contribute their unique skills and earn a major share of the revenue, which circulates in the local economy, spurring growth beyond what is considered viable by traditional market economists.

The Mongolian cashmere example inspires an opportunity for Argentina. The country has two, well-known, domesticated animals—llamas and alpacas—that contribute to niche markets with their wool. An even greater opportunity arises for two other, lesser-known members of the same camelid family: the vicuña and the guanaco.

The vicuña lives exclusively in the high mountains of the Andes. The guanaco lives in the mountains as well as in the lower lands of the Pampas Plains and Patagonia. Their presence maintains the balance and quality of fragile ecosystems, however, these wild animals have lived in symbiotic relationships with the traditional cultures of the Andes countries (Bolivia, Peru, Chile, and Argentina) for thousands of years. This harmonious relationship provides a unique opportunity since their wool provides fibers of exceptional quality. Vicuña wool provides the finest, most sought-after fiber in the world, and is in high demand of leading international fashion designers. Guanaco fibers have a similar, exclusive quality, but the wool is still over-shadowed by vicuña and alpaca. It is less known and does not carry the exclusive brand name vicuña has acquired.

The downy undercoat—the fleece—of the guanaco and vicuña makes extremely warm wool that outperforms cashmere in softness. The wool is spun into yarn and knit or woven into luxury garments. The extreme softness is caused by the narrow diameter of the fiber found close to the skin of the animals, separated from the rough overcoat in an intricate process. The wool of the animal's overcoat could be used for carpets. It is soft and hardy, having been produced through living in an extreme climate.

The vicuña and guanaco have never been farmed because they do not permit themselves to be domesticated. They maintain themselves grazing the land. They don't need to be fed or otherwise taken care of, which means they are able to provide their "wild fibers" at the cost of harvesting. It also means that, until recently, hunters (and poachers) simply shot the animals to get their wool. Unfortunately, recent growth in the guanaco population has put them in competition with sheep. The precious guanacos are chased away and/or killed en masse to make space for sheep since the wild animals had been grazing "too much." As a result, the vicuña is included on the Convention on International Trade in Endangered Species' (CITIES) list of endangered species, and the guanaco figures on the red list of the International Union for the Conservation of Nature (IUCN).

Any economic initiative with vicuña and guanaco wool needs to demonstrate proper management of the species. To capture the animals, villagers organize chakus—a gathering technique with hundreds of people chanting and driving the animals toward portable fence structures that can be set up in places where the animals are optimally concentrated. The wild animals are funneled into a central corral where they can be shorn.

It takes about three minutes to shave the animal once it has been blinded to reduce the stress involved. Afterward, they are quickly reintegrated in their wild environment.

The process requires diligent care to respect animal welfare and minimize the risk of incident. This is also critical because the CITES' protection prevents the export of products related to harming endangered species.

Peru, Bolivia, and Chile show they can produce 40 to 50 tons of vicuña and guanaco fleece per year with minimal investments. This is not a considerable quantity, as a vicuña produces only 200 grams of fleece fibers every three years. Raw vicuña wool, however, gets the highest price of fiber in the world, with 500 dollars or more per kilo. To put that into perspective: The market price of vicuña wool is almost ten times higher than the price of cashmere, and more than 100 times higher than that of sheep. This means the vicuña offer an opportunity for economic and social development for communities in Argentina's highlands that are often quite destitute.

The communities can add more value with traditional craftsmanship. In addition to the preliminary cleaning of the fiber, fabric designs integrated with silver and leather can be created. The guanaco wool has nearly the same softness but lacks the vicuña's fame, which opens the door to promotion and marketing.

At present, local communities don't fully benefit from the unique opportunities offered by vicuña wool. The raw material is purchased by Italian designers, often at below market prices of 350 dollars per kilo, and the added value of the production of fabrics and clothing is only produced abroad. The communities of vicuña lands in the Andes don't have direct access to the world market.

Our initial objective is for Argentina to develop a domestic market for vicuña wool served by highland communities. Further down the road, there is the opportunity to connect local producers with international customers ensuring—as is the case in the example of cashmere from Mongolia—that value is created and realized where it belongs and can have the most impact. The income of artisan producers should be linked to the final sale price of the products, rather than the weight of the fabrics they produce. This is a major shift: instead of selling kilos, one sells the extraordinary experience of products that last for more than a generation. This is the antithesis of fast fashion. The good news for these Argentinean communities is that the extraordinary quality of vicuña wool presents the perfect conditions for a suppliers' market. There is substantial, unsatisfied, international demand. In fact, the Hermes Foundation, based in Paris and funded by the family-controlled high-fashion company, has a broad experience in supporting the development of production in local communities, building on age-old and time-tested traditions.

The development of the small-scale industry will require limited investments in the chaku-capturing structures, which the communities are already assuming. The missing links are the local spinning facilities. Vicuña and guanaco fibers are very soft, but they are also very short. This means they need to be processed in a non-static environment. Traditionally, the yarn is manufactured following ancient techniques with simple, inexpensive, wooden spinning instruments.

Five years ago, there were only 120,000 vicuña left in Argentina, however, their numbers are rising. It is estimated there are now some 300,000 vicuña. This means that 100,000 vicuña can be shorn each year, and at an average of 200 grams of fleece wool per animal, the annual harvest can be as much as three tons. There are six million guanacos in Argentina, and they can potentially provide 400 tons of wool per year. The initial focus is on 600,000 guanacos that can provide 40 tons of wool per year for an income of up to 20 million dollars. Add another five million for the quality fleece produced and transformed by local communities in the north of the Province of Jujuy.

Between the vicuña and guanaco, Argentina could produce wild fibers for some 25 million dollars in revenue. This amount rises when more local value is added, and when the number of animals increases. Still, the projected income doesn't change much in the mindset of government offices in Buenos Aires, where this initiative may be considered too small to deserve high-level attention, however, it has the potential to transform nine Coya communities at four- to 5,000-meter altitudes in the high mountains bordering Bolivia, especially when we realize that the restoration of a traditional culture and local economy can be a starting point for new activities. The highlands of Argentina offer exceptional natural beauty in the form of unique rock-color formations and sub-soil glaciers that few have been able to appreciate. With the distribution of the fine vicuña wool through the high-end global fashion market, an interest in the region of origin could be developed. Every piece that is produced links back to the highlands where the vicuña roam. The investment in this exceptional product is converted into an opportunity for private "vicuña safaris." Eco-tourism with respect for local environment and communities can kick-start a multiplier effect with the initial revenue of 25 million dollars of vicuña (and guanaco) hair turning into a 100 million dollar travel industry, bypassing the income generated today by the wool industry.

This development also supports the environment. Without new and better opportunities, the local population has ventured into cow farming, sold as "insurance," as there is always a good demand for Argentine meat that has roamed freely in the highlands. Cows, however, are too heavy for the fragile soil on top of the underground glaciers, which suffer from the urine. This means the glaciers—which are already under stress from climate change—will disintegrate even faster, releasing massive amounts of methane, the greenhouse gas that has about 30 times more impact than carbon dioxide when it comes to global

Plan A

warming. Moreover, the cow transmits skin diseases that could affect the quality and the long-term harvesting of vicuña wool. Native vicuña, on the other hand, sustains the ecosystem. A better local economy around the vicuña allows for the removal of cattle from this vulnerable ecosystem. There is also the opportunity to regenerate vicuña herds. Presently, there are a few hundred thousand of them, but it is estimated that the ecosystem can easily carry a million or even more. In the past, the vicuña were sacrificed for short-term gain, whereas the guanaco was killed for its meat. Today, Argentina has a great opportunity to regenerate the ecosystem, which goes, in this case, hand in hand with a revival of culture and tradition while building up regional economic development centered around a product with a story that speaks to the imagination—the softest wool on the planet. The production and trade of wild fibers integrated with ecotourism shows there are ways for local communities to compete in a global market with limited investment and the uplifting of a region that has been too dependent on government aid for too long. Investors have the desire to take this initiative to the next level.

The Transformation of Argentina's Economy

Clustering culture with tradition and fibers

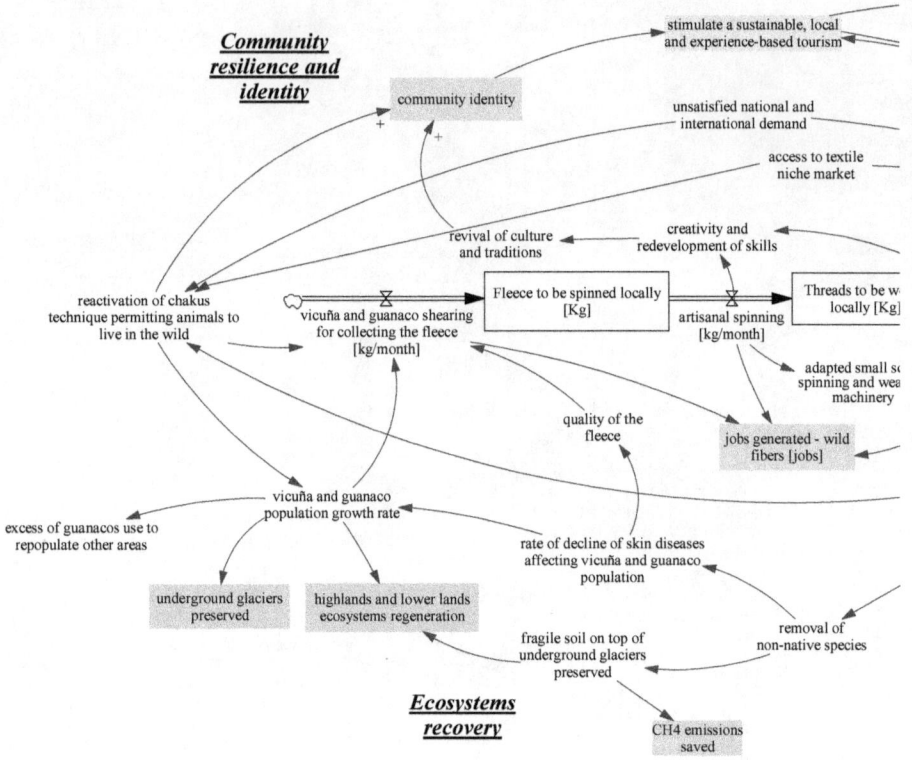

The Transformation of Argentina's Economy

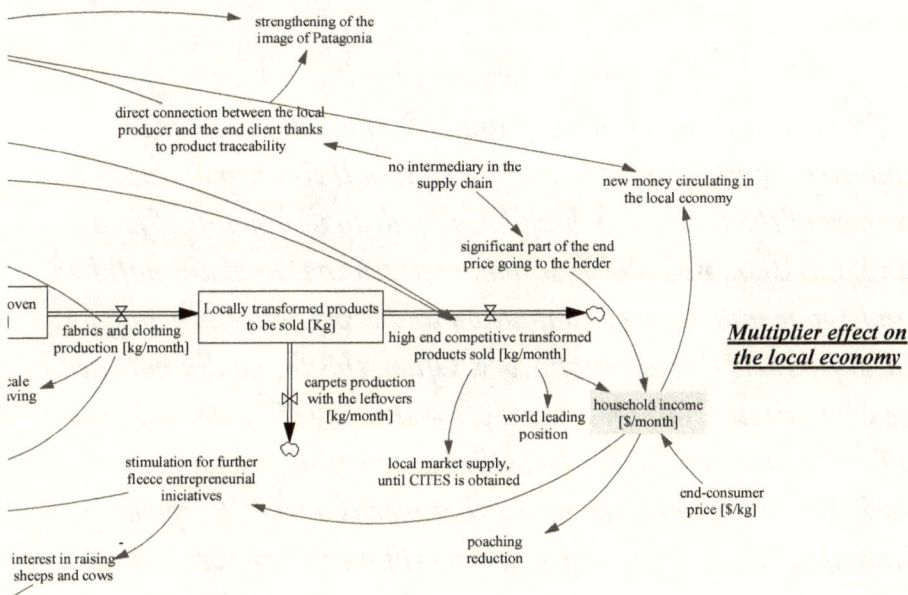

strengthening of the
image of Patagonia

direct connection between the local
producer and the end client thanks
to product traceability

no intermediary in the
supply chain

new money circulating in
the local economy

significant part of the end
price going to the herder

oven

fabrics and clothing
production [kg/month]

Locally transformed products
to be sold [Kg]

high end competitive transformed
products sold [kg/month]

:ale
iving

carpets production
with the leftovers
[kg/month]

world leading
position

household income
[$/month]

*Multiplier effect on
the local economy*

stimulation for further
fleece entrepreneurial
iniciatives

local market supply,
until CITES is obtained

end-consumer
price [$/kg]

interest in raising
sheeps and cows

poaching
reduction

Fable 8
A fleece jacket

Cows have turned into the standards of the milk and meat industry. While European emigrants took their animals to the four corners of the world searching for a predictable amount of food and nutrition, newcomers seldom realized that local animals had undergone millennia of adaptation and evolution, ending up as ideal partners throughout history. Often, this fauna did not need to be domesticated. On the contrary, the strategy of "catch and release" offered all the benefits without the burden of maintenance and feed. This is a time-tested model that merits a revisit, especially since it offers an opportunity in a world market of over-supply to offer a few unique products and experiences unparalleled in the world.

It is cold and windy. A vicuña is roaming the highlands of Argentina, close to the border with Bolivia when it spots a cow.

"You must have lost your way. Shall I show you how to get back down to the valley?" wonders the vicuña.

"That is very kind of you. I realize you are not only a very elegant inhabitant of the mountains but that you are courteous, as well," responds the cow.

"You must be freezing cold. You aren't very well-dressed for up here."

"I really don't want to be here. I'm suffering. The air is so thin that I can hardly breathe. Sadly, they will not let me get back to where I belong."

"Who holds you hostage?"

"Well, these white people put me on ships and made me travel from far away. That was stressful. Then, I was sent up these hills."

"Hills? You are on top of the world. And, if you are not dressed right for this, you will suffer, get sick, and eventually die."

"How come you are so well-dressed for this hardship?"

"Hardship? This is my home. Look: I got a fleece jacket underneath my wool that keeps me very warm."

"A fleece jacket? What a great invention. I thought Patagonia made it up."

"The people who have lived here since early times shave off my fleece in the spring to make the finest clothing that will protect them through icy winters."

"They shave you? They did not kill you for your hide?"

"Ah, no. We have lived in harmony for 10,000 years. The people considered us the goddesses of the Andes. The first woven clothing ever on earth comes from tiny little fibers than can only be made by us."

"And the softest! Compare your wool to anything. You even make cashmere feel coarse."

"We do not make wool. We make fleece, and the kings of the world desired us. They loved us so much, they left us to roam in the wild and never forced us into a corral until the colonizers arrived and wanted cows."

"Why can't I dress up like you? Why can't I run free like you?"

Plan A

"Because everyone needs a millennia to adjust to life at a place before it turns into a home. By the way, your hoofs are too big, and you are too heavy. You damage our fragile soil and destroy the ice underneath."

"I'm sorry. I realize this is certainly not my home. I gasp for air, my feet get cold, my nose itches, and I sneeze all the time."

"Just let us hope that when you leave for home, you don't pass by a slaughterhouse, or you may be turned into a sausage before you know it."

... And it only has just begun!

The Transformation of Argentina's Economy

Plan A

Argentinian Map of Opportunities

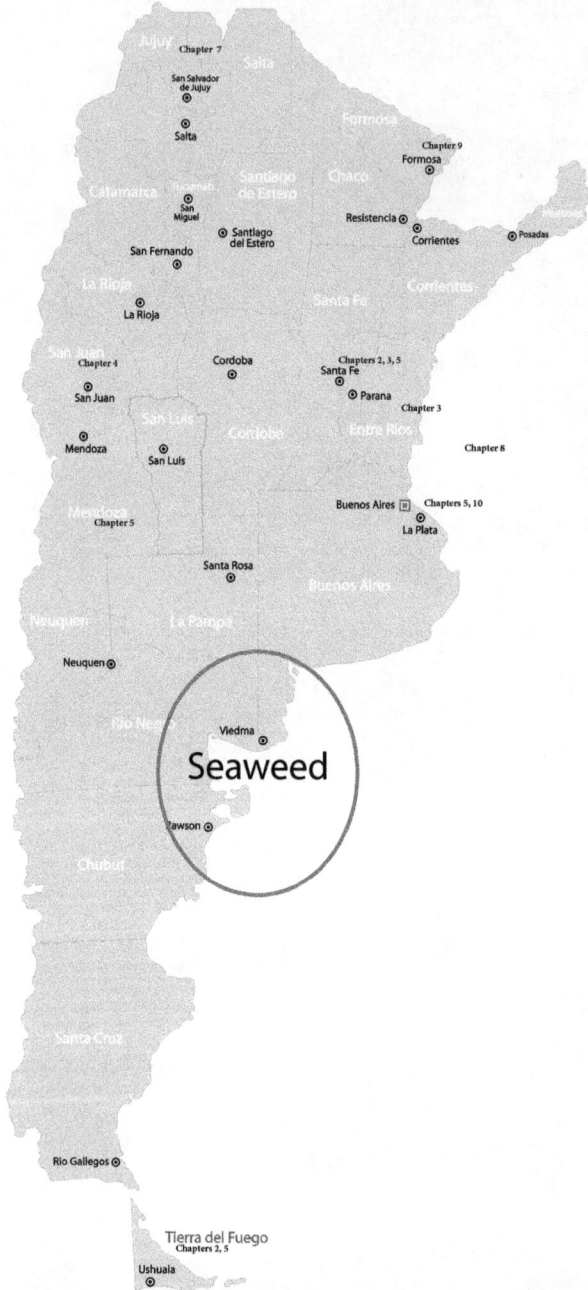

PART C

Transformation of the Energy Economy

Plan A

Chapter 8

From Fracking Soil to Farming in 3D

G overnments worldwide face big challenges to transform their energy economies. The fossil fuels determining energy policies for over a century are being phased out, but they still provide the lion's share of energy needs. As the Norwegian Statoil board stated, "There are alternatives, but oil is here to stay for decades to come." Wind and solar are fast emerging as the energy sources of the future, however, these renewable sources require a new and very different infrastructure. This means large-scale investments for which money is not readily available, so governments are caught between the urgent need to prepare for change and their inability to quickly write off past investments while ensuring the lights stay on at the same time.

In this context, Argentina faces a unique dilemma. For decades, the country has supplied neighboring countries with natural gas, however, over the past ten years, as reserves were exhausted, the gas pipelines started to flow in a reverse direction, and the country turned from a net exporter of gas into a net importer from Chile and Bolivia. Today, Argentina imports expensive gas by maritime transport from the overseas spot-market to fuel the country's energy needs. A power cut is the worst scenario a politician in office can experience.

The substitution of cheap, local power with imported fuel comes at a hefty price, draining Argentina of billions of dollars each year. This is why the Argentine government has set out on a course to secure the country's future energy sources. Given the existing gas infrastructure, the most logical next step seemed to be the exploration of Argentina's vast shale reserves through fracking, particularly in Patagonia. The government entered into negotiations with big, international players, like Chevron and Total, who stand ready to make large investments in shale gas exploration. The price setting—based on demand and substitution cost of imports—is high, securing steady and solid profits for investors.

Anyone who has visited the marvels of Patagonia understands the dilemma Argentina faces. Yes, the country needs cheaper, locally available energy, and with an abundant supply ready to be fracked and cracked, why would anyone so emotional as to prohibit the obvious? At the same time, it is hard to imagine that Patagonia's natural beauty might be sacrificed for this goal. The gas industry does not have a clean record when it comes to fracking. According to a recent study in the journal Environmental Science and Technology, dumping fracking water into rivers, lakes, and streams can cause lasting environmental damage, even if the water is treated first.

Shale gas is not the preferred choice of the industry; it

has been estimated that to be competitive, shale gas needs a minimum oil price of 50 dollars per barrel. Fracking was an extraordinary business when oil traded above 100 dollars per barrel for years, however, recent developments in the oil market make shale gas much less attractive and hardly a reliable investment for the future, despite the interests shown by oil giants such as Chevron and Total. It works when politics are in favor—in spite of environmental and cost concerns—or when local demand largely exceeds supply. Argentina complies with these requisites.

Even in the best scenarios, the future of shale gas is limited due to the economics. It requires the collusion of accounting rules and permit arrangements to become an attractive investment. Forty percent of any newly explored reserves is extracted in the first year of operation; 25 percent in the second year; and 15 percent in the third year. In other words, 80 percent of the reserves are pulled out in the first three years of operation. This makes the investment interesting from a financial perspective, as high initial costs are recouped within three years. This return on investment is easy to finance and hard to refuse. It also makes it attractive for a government keen on providing a quick solution to a complex situation— the reserves are abundant, the technologies are proven, the damage is known, the financing is available, and the deployment is as fast as permits can be issued.

There is, however, a caveat. After the return on investment is made in three years, the remaining 20 percent of the reserves are left untouched. With a 20-year license, the gas companies keep the reserves on their balance sheets for another 17 years.

As their stock market valuation is substantially based on their access to proven reserves, these shine in the eyes of investors. This is an important accounting exercise since it means the books boost reserves. It also means the cleanup of the environment will only happen—and be paid for—after 20 (or perhaps 17) years. The full costs are not immediately put on the books since the discounted amount would be considered too small, and the exact amount too uncertain. This means the closure costs don't impact profit margins, making the investment even more attractive. In the meantime, societies are left with a lot of uncertainty about the environmental damage and who will remediate it.

In addition, one day, the remaining reserves will be sold off to another party, and the clean-up bill will somehow get lost in the transaction. Alberta, the pioneer province of shale gas and fracking in Canada, offers terrifying testimony of these practices.

Argentina finds itself in a complex, unfortunate situation. The country has high debts and faces high import costs for energy. It has a multi-billion-dollar gas pipeline infrastructure and some of the largest shale gas reserves in the world.

Despite the high environmental "externalized" costs, development of shale gas seems the only reasonable option.

Unless there's a better alternative…

Yes, Argentina should continue to power its economy with gas, however, the country has the great opportunity to harvest the gas from seaweed plantations along its long coastline in an immaculate and renewable way with many externalized *benefits*. You read that correctly: instead of external costs, this energy model generates external benefits. This is the key element of the new rules of an economy in transformation.

Argentina has 3.3 million square kilometers of territorial seas. A team of 14 local scientists headed by Prof. Dr. Elisa Parodi from the National University of the South in Bahia Blanca estimates that one-third of this area—about one million square kilometers—is good for farming seaweed. One might agree that 10% is ideal; it is still good for a whopping 100,000 km². The ocean along the country's coast is not very deep, and the water temperature is optimal for seaweed cultivation. In fact, Argentina was the world's largest exporter of seaweed until the early 1970s, harvested and sold around the world for use in fertilizer and as an animal feed additive. The Argentine seaweed sector died when natural gas replaced seaweed as the resource for synthetic fertilizers. The country has also lost its interest in the labor-intensive process and discovered the ease of export of protein from meat and soy based on an abundance of land.

Today, seaweed offers a new opportunity and the basis for a major transformation of the energy economy. Recent tests conducted by seaweed farming expert INRADA from the Netherlands off the coast of Cape Town in South Africa has demonstrated that one hectare of seaweed can produce—over two production cycles of six months—as much as 1,000 tons per year. That biomass of 1,000 tons can be converted into 200,000 cubic meters of gas per year, or 548 cubic meters of gas per day, for 365 days a year. Similar results were produced in experiments in Indonesia. A successful shale gas field in the United States is happy with an output of 6,000 cubic meters per hour, or some 50 million cubic meters per year, and the field produces gas for three years; 250 hectares, or 2.5 square kilometers, of seaweed can replace the production of this shale gas field, every year, forever (that is, as long as the sun shines and there is water in the ocean).

If Argentina farms seaweed on one million square kilometers—one-third of its territorial seas—it can generate 40 billion tons of seaweed annually or an "eternal supply" of 8,000 billion cubic meters of gas. This outpaces any reserve of any gas field anywhere in the world.

The seaweed plantation of one million square kilometers will sequester 4.5 billion ton CO_2 each year.

The potential of seaweed gas is massive. The United States could fulfill its entire, annual energy needs with a seaweed farm of 650,000 square kilometers—that's less than the Argentinean capacity of one million square kilometers. By comparison, today farmers cultivate 3.7 million square kilometers of land in the US.

The productivity of seaweed can be explained by the fact that farming in the sea happens in a three-dimensional environment. The seaweed can easily grow three meters deep, unaffected by gravity and is able to reach depths of 25 meters. This allows for a volume and a speed of the conversion of solar energy that is impossible to achieve when farming in a two-dimensional environment on land. In addition, water is 784 times denser than air and supplies multiple nutrients per cubic meter. The productivity levels of three-dimensional farming in the sea lies beyond the reach of the most advanced genetics and chemical cocktails. This is not a matter of for or against—

this is a matter of the laws of physics determining dimension and density.

The harvested seaweed is washed and processed so that the cells rupture and are enriched with hydrogen. Now, it can be fermented, and new technology makes it possible to efficiently generate methane at scale. Producing biogas through the fermentation of seaweed in a digester is a simple process compared to, for instance, converting corn into ethanol, which is a capital-intensive, chemical process. The pre-processing of seaweed before the digestion and the use of 12 chambers for the processing increases the conversion of the biomass into methane (CH_4) to 90 percent and cuts the retention time to eight to nine days. This increases the efficiency of biomass from the sea compared to any other source by a factor of 50, which is disruptive.

There is another factor making seaweed as a source for biogas very compelling: the infrastructure. Argentina, like most countries, has an existing infrastructure of natural gas pipelines. This means that a transition to biogas from seaweed will not require massive, infrastructural investments, as an equally potent gas will flow through the same pipes. This makes seaweed very attractive as a source of power, even when compared to the rapid rise of wind and solar. This appeals to the Captains of Legacy who, through their family offices, monitor these developments vigilantly. The only thing required is the adaptation of the gas to specifications required for pipeline transmissions. This is not a problem. Shale from fracking requires a similar adaptation.

Seaweed does need some infrastructure, though. The weeds

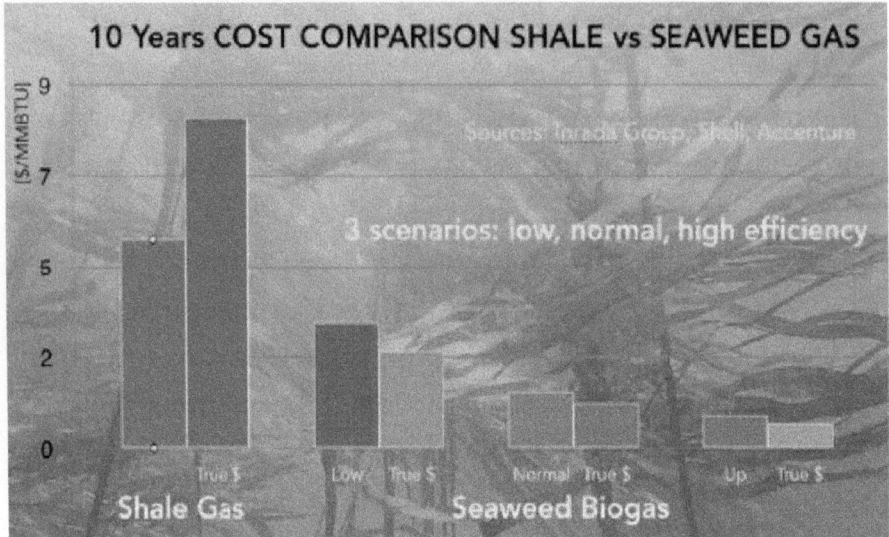

10 Years COST COMPARISON SHALE vs SEAWEED GAS

Sources: Inrada Group, Shell, Accenture

3 scenarios: low, normal, high efficiency

Shale Gas   Seaweed Biogas

can be cultivated on platforms using the same buoyancy science as the ones developed by the oil industry for offshore oil exploration that will be placed along the coast in a modular way at an investment of 25,000 dollars per hectare (2.5 million dollars per square kilometer). A greater challenge will be the digester infrastructure, but its cost is already included in the ballpark, 25,000 number. The digestion process, as described above, is simple, however, the process needs to be scaled to a level at which it can feed Argentina's vast infrastructure of gas pipelines. This is a different order of magnitude from digesting biomass into biogas at a piggery farm. This project requires a management team is capable of going to scale with speed.

We need to imagine digester parks in zones close to harvesting points in order to reduce transportation costs. Still, investing in seaweed biogas over a ten-year period is much more efficient than investing in shale gas, as the graph above shows. Shale gas can only be competitive at around 50 dollars per barrel; seaweed gas can be produced for six to eight dollars per barrel.

There are two other major reasons why seaweed energy potential outcompetes shale gas through fracking. Shale gas is a limited resource; the supply will end, sooner or later. On the other hand, seaweed gas can be harvested forever. Investments made today and maintained over time will produce eternal returns. Seaweed gas is a truly clean and renewable resource; there are no "closure costs" but there are operational expenses that will only decrease as experience is gained.

Secondly, we are used to economic activity and business having unwanted side-effects. We call these unintended consequences "externalized costs." Despite the fact that (most) companies carry closure costs for their harmful activities on their balance sheets (by law), these are usually costs society has to bear in terms of environmental degradation or compromised public health.

The exploration of shale gas is a clear example of an activity that comes with high external costs. By expert verification, the cost of the production of shale gas is about 5.2 dollars per million BTU, whereas the total cost, including all risks and damages plus compensation and restoration, would push it above eight dollars. By comparison, the exploration of seaweed gas comes with externalized benefits: (un)intended, beneficial side-effects. This means the cost drops per unit of energy since there are additional incomes and the power to regenerate the dynamics of an ecosystem.

After digestion of the seaweed biomass into gas, two percent of the original, wet-based weight remains. That byproduct of the digestion is an ideal fertilizer. Remember: Argentina currently also imports natural gas to produce fertilizer! The seaweed biomass will also provide a great source of animal feed—seaweed can replace the soy plantations that have depleted vast areas of agricultural soils for our growing meat consumption.

Moreover, part of the seaweed production can be used for additional, lucrative, business activities. Nearly all processed and frozen foods around the world include seaweed extracts to maintain softness and texture. Seaweed extracts, such as agar-agar and carrageenan, are key ingredients in products like toothpaste, ice cream, and cosmetic creams and lotions.

Seaweed farming can also provide fibers for the textile industry. In the 1940s, British scientists had already discovered that fibers from seaweed could be used as non-toxic, non-irritating, biodegradable woven material to treat wounds. Seaweed-based gauze has an anti-inflammatory capacity, as well, while maintaining a certain degree of humidity, supporting wound healing.

Since the early 2000s, advanced technologies have introduced seaweed fiber into the production of apparel—mostly in knits, underwear, and sportswear. As the technology improves, seaweed clothing and towels will rapidly become an alternative for cotton that drains water resources and pollutes them with toxins. Note: cultivating seaweed doesn't require water. In fact, farming seaweed produces fresh water that can be used in the industrial processes that unfold as new industrial clusters emerge, as a byproduct. Companies like Lensing in Austria have pioneered this technology in Europe, but the first examples are from Qingdao in China, where millions of units of towels have already been made with fibers derived from seaweed.

Possibly the most game-changing element of seaweed cultivation is its contribution to the environment. Fracking and fossil fuel exploitation *degrade* the environment. These activities damage nature and the name of the game is to mitigate the impact; seaweed cultivation *regenerates* nature. It is very alkaline and maintains critical pH levels in the oceans at 8.2, helping to avert the dangerous drop to 8.1 and below, leading to the destruction of coral reefs and the inability of shells to form. Moreover, since dragnet fishing has erased life on the bottom of the sea, there is the urgent need to regenerate the biodiversity of the sea. Once there is an abundance of seaweed—the precursors of life in the ocean— sponges and seashells will nestle in, and fish will settle in zones in which they feel protected from predators. The right conditions to farm oysters, abalone, mussels, or crustaceans will emerge, as well, according to the local biota that has to be kept free of invasive and non-native species.

As the marine environment regenerates, fish stocks— severely depleted from overfishing—will be restored. The beauty of the three-dimensional ecosystem of the sea is that it doesn't need any input, be it irrigation, fertilizers, or pesticides; the living organisms will feed themselves.

Research has shown how critical seafood is for our health. Omega-3 fatty acids from algae—that we can eat directly or through fish, especially through anchovies and herring who feed on sea plants—have been linked to better brain and heart health in many studies. We need healthy seas, and seaweed cultivation is the first step toward restoring the oceans' ecosystem.

In other words, seaweed generates multiple, sustainable industries with parallel revenue streams operating within the ecosystem. Seaweed cultivation will redesign major sectors of the economy trapped in conventional fossil fuel energy logic. On top of this, seaweed sequesters carbon dioxide. Some varieties absorb five times more CO_2 than land-based plants. If electricity is generated from seaweed, it will only emit 11 grams of carbon per kilowatt-hour, taking into account the building of the infrastructure. The average, other energy sources for electricity emit more than 500 grams per kWh.

Given the wide-ranging and compelling advantages of seaweed cultivation, it comes as no surprise that innovative seaweed initiatives have been undertaken around the globe. Indonesia is building a 100 MW energy plant that will be completely powered by seaweed. Belgium is contemplating seaweed farming as part of a new initiative to protect its coastal zone against climate change. Recently, the US government, after first concluding that a multi-million dollar subsidy program for the production of ethanol from corn had reached its end, awarded a series of contracts to stimulate the cultivation of seaweed for the production of biogas.

Argentina has a great opportunity to join this seaweed-driven wave to transform an energy economy that has dominated societies for over a century. With a modest investment of 25,000 dollars per platform, Argentina can substitute the import of natural gas over between 18 and 24 months with domestic biogas production. Within five years, it will be possible to replace gas imports from neighboring countries, which will save Argentina billions of dollars annually.

There are challenges to overcome. The two zones selected for the first 100 square kilometers of seaweed farms don't have enough people living on the coasts to provide the necessary labor, as local seaweed cultivation was abandoned some 40 years. The digester technology needs to be scaled, and the know-how must be transferred. Argentina needs to change the law prohibiting the distribution of biogas—which—typically includes corrosive elements, through existing, natural gas pipelines. Seaweed-derived gas, however, has an extremely low level of hydrogen sulfide (H_2S)—much less than shale gas contains—which is now permitted to be distributed through the existing infrastructure. Corrosion gases have been addressed in the digester technology, but the old law singling out biogas is still in place. Finally, shale gas investments—about 15 million dollars per well—are typically financed by one major gas multinational. Seaweed cultivation requires smaller investments that have to come from multiple, smaller companies, but with a guaranteed demand at a competitive price, this will be a lucrative opportunity. In fact, the first established seaweed farm can produce sufficient income to finance ten (!) new ones, able to generate biomass as long as the sun shines and there's water in the ocean.

Seaweed farming is a global game-changer. Argentina is ideally positioned to present itself as an early pioneer and leader in this field, showing there's a better energy future than devastating natural beauty through fracking to produce shale gas. The list of advantages and benefits is long and compelling: seaweed cultivation is more efficient than shale gas exploration; and it provides an endless energy source, whereas shale gas resources will eventually be exhausted. Not only can seaweed substitute natural gas imports, but it can also deliver organic fertilizer that can be distributed using the existing natural gas infrastructure (the same applies to shale gas). Seaweed cultivation protects Patagonia's natural beauty while regenerating the marine ecosystem along Argentina's coast, which will support the restoration of fish stocks. Once the coastal zones recover as a result of seaweed forests, they will temper the waves and protect coastal zones against rising sea levels while sequestering carbon and helping to mitigate climate change as a zero-emissions energy source. Finally, seaweed cultivation offers multiple additional benefits from animal feed to ingredients for the textile, food, and cosmetics industries.

We are standing at the beginning of an energy revolution. Seaweed cultivation doesn't compare with anything we have had before, and this is why a new generation of investors is required, pioneers who we have labeled Captains of Legacy. It will inspire generations of scientists and entrepreneurs to come with opportunities to fuel and feed societies in sustainable and renewable ways. This is an extraordinary opportunity for Argentina and for leaders and investors in the country who want to transform the economy and put the nation on a true path of sustainable development. All of this while responding to the basic needs of all with what is available within the existing carrying capacity while offering a solid and continuous return with low risk, provided the entrepreneurs operate with speed and reach a scale to impact the country and change the statistics, once and for all.

Clustering seaweed with gas and fertilizers

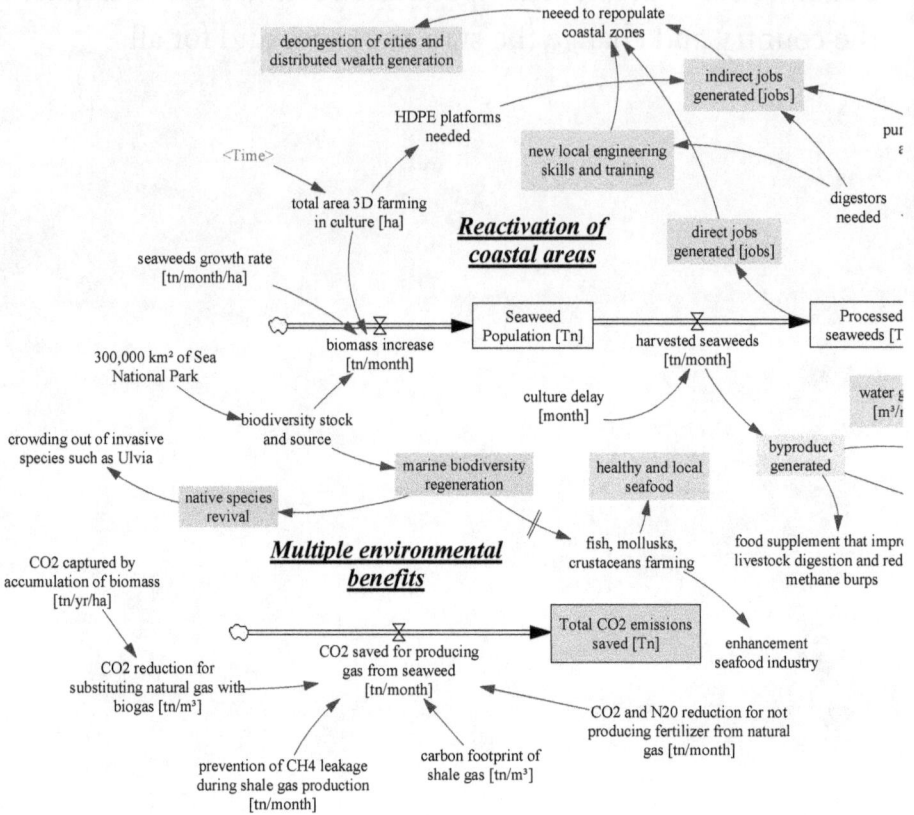

neeed to repopulate coastal zones

decongestion of cities and distributed wealth generation

indirect jobs generated [jobs]

pur

HDPE platforms needed

new local engineering skills and training

<Time>

total area 3D farming in culture [ha]

digestors needed

Reactivation of coastal areas

direct jobs generated [jobs]

seaweeds growth rate [tn/month/ha]

300,000 km² of Sea National Park

biomass increase [tn/month]

Seaweed Population [Tn]

harvested seaweeds [tn/month]

Processed seaweeds [T

culture delay [month]

water [m³/

biodiversity stock and source

crowding out of invasive species such as Ulvia

marine biodiversity regeneration

healthy and local seafood

byproduct generated

native species revival

Multiple environmental benefits

fish, mollusks, crustaceans farming

food supplement that impr livestock digestion and red methane burps

CO2 captured by accumulation of biomass [tn/yr/ha]

CO2 saved for producing gas from seaweed [tn/month]

Total CO2 emissions saved [Tn]

enhancement seafood industry

CO2 reduction for substituting natural gas with biogas [tn/m³]

CO2 and N20 reduction for not producing fertilizer from natural gas [tn/month]

prevention of CH4 leakage during shale gas production [tn/month]

carbon footprint of shale gas [tn/m³]

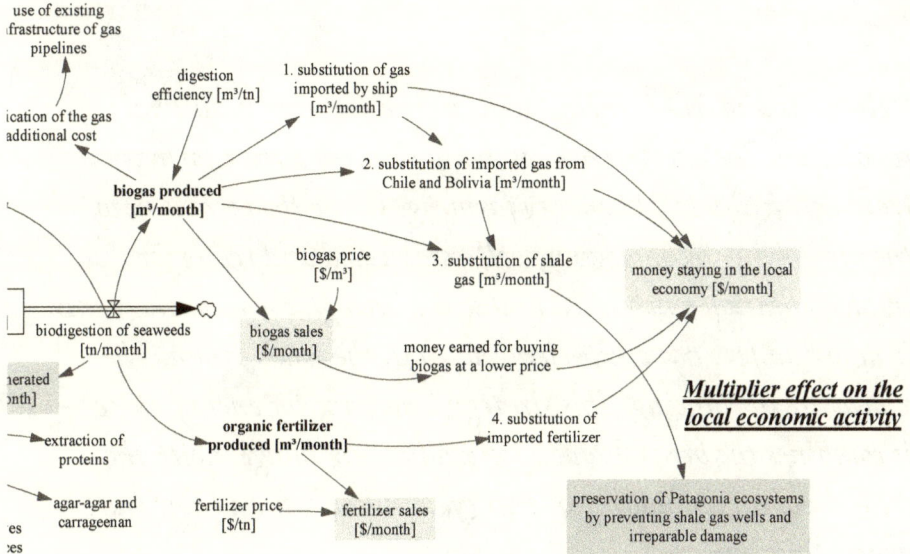

use of existing
infrastructure of gas
pipelines

digestion
efficiency [m³/tn]

1. substitution of gas
imported by ship
[m³/month]

ication of the gas
additional cost

2. substitution of imported gas from
Chile and Bolivia [m³/month]

**biogas produced
[m³/month]**

biogas price
[$/m³]

3. substitution of shale
gas [m³/month]

money staying in the local
economy [$/month]

biodigestion of seaweeds
[tn/month]

biogas sales
[$/month]

money earned for buying
biogas at a lower price

ierated
nth]

extraction of
proteins

**organic fertilizer
produced [m³/month]**

4. substitution of
imported fertilizer

*__Multiplier effect on the
local economic activity__*

agar-agar and
carrageenan

es
es

fertilizer price
[$/tn]

fertilizer sales
[$/month]

preservation of Patagonia ecosystems
by preventing shale gas wells and
irreparable damage

Fable 9
Adding a dimension

Robotics and 3D printing will inspire the next industrial revolution. The energy sector is going through a transformation from extraction to 3D energy farming. While the term is new, the underlying technology is well-established and ready for implementation with speed and scale. Though the technology mix is new and few have experience with it, the trials around the world are convincing. This strategy is not one for energy alone— it combines the breakthrough for eradicating hunger with the creation of an abundance of energy, at a low cost and without generating emissions.

A fly was listening in on a conversation of people and shares what it overheard with a silverfish. It is all about a new machine.

"Everyone in the office is so excited about this 3D printer, no one even bothered chasing after me," says the fly.

"I do not get excited about this machine. It spews strange gases and seems to use a lot of plastics."

"Nothing is perfect from day one. You need to display some patience and learn from this novelty. Eventually, everything can take a turn for the better."

"I admire your positive approach, but I am worried this printer will be just a toy, create a lot of hype and discussion, cut jobs, and divert all attention away from the real challenges the world faces."

"I did not know you were interested in the troubles we all face. What stresses you out the most?"

"It is time that we find a solution for food. There is simply not enough food, and what we eat is mostly rubbish. Where are the good old days when everything was organic and natural?"

"That was back then when there were only one billion people on Earth. Do you realize what it means to feed ten billion mouths?"

"We have heard that before, and as more and more people populate a limited space, we keep on farming in 2D."

"What do you mean: farming in two dimensions?"

"If we are not embracing three dimensions and tackling more problems all at once, we will never shift from scarcity to abundance."

"You are out of your mind! With ten billion people to feed, we can never eradicate hunger and poverty, let alone dream about abundance for all."

"I beg to differ. Instead of all this buzz about 3D printers, why is there no buzz about 3D farming?"

"I have never heard of that! It sounds like magic to me!"

"Magic? When a rainforest produces biomass, is that in two or three dimensions?"

"Deep forests have high trees and different bushes of all sizes, so it is 3D."

"And kelp growing in the sea with the sponges and shells, is that two or 3D?"

"It's obviously 3D."

"So why are we worried about how many crops are

produced per acre? Time has come to see how many tons we can produce in all the space that we have."

"You are so right! Farming in the sea offers ten times more space than on land, and no one has to work against gravity."

"The time has come to do better, forever regenerating the space, using the nutrients we have and nothing else, and hunger will be a thing of the past."

... And it only has just begun!

The Transformation of Argentina's Economy

Plan A

Argentinian Map of Opportunities

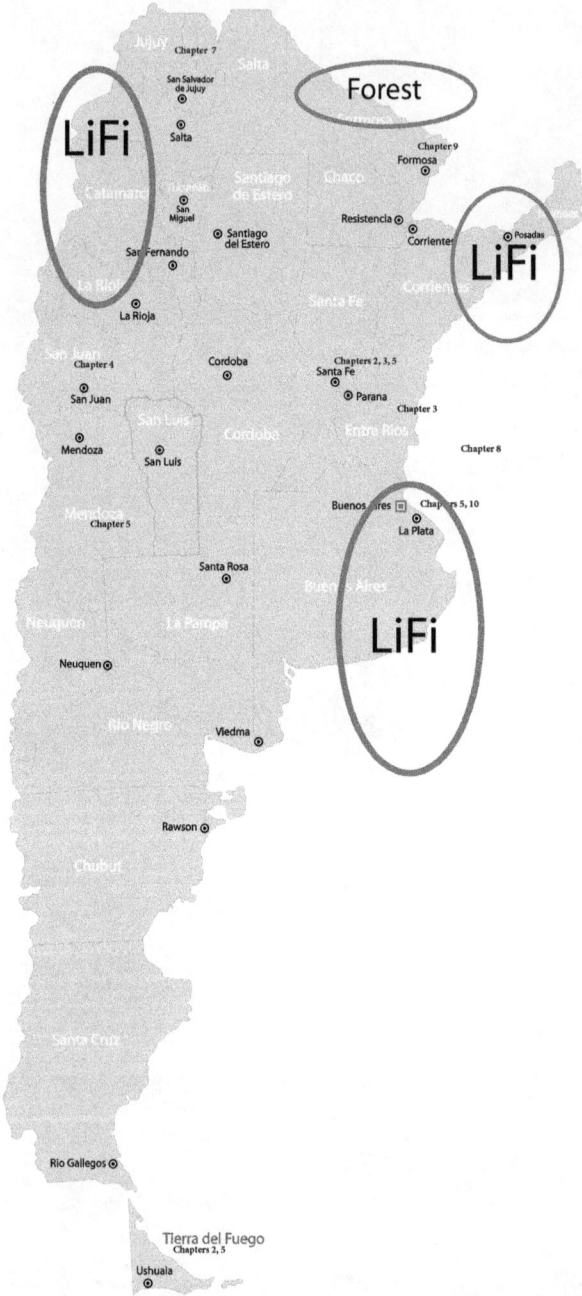

PART D

Reaching
the
Unreached

Plan A

Chapter 9

Reaching full employment converting savanna to forest

E very second, some 500 trees, which take, on average, 20 years to become fully grown, are cut on the planet. That is 15 billion trees every year. Most of these trees are cut to make space to grow more food. It is sad and painful that the planet is still losing valuable forest cover which protects the soil from drying out; it is even sadder and more painful that deforestation ultimately hampers the very agriculture and food supply for which the trees make way. Over 50 percent of the planet's tree cover has been lost in an unrelenting process that is like pulling off the skin from the Earth—not only does it hurt, but after a while, there is no way you can continue to support the same living conditions without trees. Europe is the only continent where the number of trees is continually increasing.

According to the Food and Agriculture Organization of the United Nations (FAO), Argentina is among the top ten destructive countries when it comes to their forests. The FAO calculates the loss at eight million hectares since 1990. Over almost three decades, Argentina's forest cover decreased from 13 percent of the country's landmass to ten.

Plan A

Eighty percent of the deforestation takes place in the northeastern part of the country. This is where Douglas and Kris Tompkins, in collaboration with Georges Soros and Harvard University, started a conservation project with the aim of preserving and strengthening the 553,000 hectares of Iberá Provincial Natural Reserve in the Province of Corrientes, founded in 1983. The project acquired 150,000 hectares of old cattle ranches bordering the existing natural reserve. The goal is to help these lands transition from "an exploitative economy" to "an economy of conservation and ecotourism" before they are returned to the Argentine government to be included in the reserve to create the largest national park in Argentina, 700,000 hectares in size.

The Tompkins' initiative helps, but at the same time, satellite data continues to confirm a clear link between areas planted with soybeans and the deforestation of native Argentinean forests. Taking away the trees creates vast, accessible, easily be plowed fields. This starts monoculture farming, intended to produce the highest possible yields using chemistry—fertilizers, herbicides, fungicides, and pesticides—and genetics (GMOs). The problem is that we have been ignoring the laws of physics determining the delicate balance between water and sun, but as it turns out, we cannot ultimately defy physics with chemistry and genetics. Plan A builds on several strategic opportunities embedded in the transformation of protein and energy supply, which could reach a whole new order of magnitude—far beyond the promise of fast-growing trees—when we shift the business model, so it follows the laws of physics. This is a critical framework in order to understand the emerging investment opportunity, discussed for the Province of Formosa.

There's another reason why we have to make this shift. When we expose the soil directly to the blazing sun, ultraviolet rays sanitize it; the sun kills the nutrients the plants need, so we need more chemicals to replenish what we have lost, and we cannot regenerate the ecosystem without re-creating the shade. Exposure to the sun also makes sure the temperature of the soil will rise so it will become warmer than the rain. This means that when the rain hits the soil, the water will immediately evaporate and the morning dew will be gone before it can benefit the plants as the water won't get a chance to penetrate the soil and feed the crops.

There is no canopy of trees above the field able to catch the water and cascade it gradually back into the underground, streams, and rivers. This will lead to a free fall of raindrops, and torrential rains will wreak havoc on exposed soil, increasing erosion and reducing water absorption capacities. We will dry out the land in search of a higher level of productivity and then need irrigation—including the energy required to pump the water and the pipes that channel the water—to the point of consumption. This process of irrigation creates an over-mineralization of the soil, putting the wrong mix of minerals into the ground, gradually making the soil infertile. It also creates a kind of "stone" layer, ensuring that heavy rains—when the water won't evaporate right away—provoke flooding. The flooding will wash away the debris of decomposing biomass that should have provided the nutrients for the next harvest, and we enter into a cycle of adding more and more fertilizers. In order to reduce the costs of the destruction of water and temperature cycles, there are increasing calls for new genetics, plants resisting the uncertainties created by our drive to maximize output.

This is exactly what we have seen happening throughout Argentina. The productivity of farming goes down, yields drop, and costs increase, reducing margins. The use of chemicals constrains the export opportunity, especially since the European Union has imposed stringent limits on residual traces of agro-chemicals. This means export has shifted to China, which pays lower prices.

In other words, the simple misunderstanding of how physics works leads to deforestation and ultimately, to desertification. Even shorter: cutting trees to make space for agriculture leads to less food and more hunger over a period of two to three decades. We need trees because they stand at the core of the ecosystem, and the natural cover that emerged over millennia contributes to the composition of the atmosphere on which human life depends. Trees are the skin of the earth, and it is about time we take their presence seriously—at least if we want to feed the world. There is no better proof for the vital presence of trees and their predominant role in transforming business and society than the story of Las Gaviotas in Colombia. This is the model we propose Argentina emulate.

In 1967, Paolo Lugari founded a village in the Vichada region of the Orinoco River in the eastern savannas of Colombia. It was an area where no one thought anything could grow, as the Spanish conquistadores had cut down the last trees 250 years prior. Fifteen million acres of land lost tree coverage long before deforestation in the Amazon rainforest gained international attention. The soil and the water had turned acidic, and 70 percent of the remaining population— out of a mere 26,000 people—suffered from gastrointestinal illnesses. The land is exposed to the scorching sun for nine months of the year, while torrential rains make life very difficult during the remaining three months. Chemistry and genetics had no effect on the degeneration of the land, and the region suffered the highest infant death and unemployment rates in Colombia.

Lugari, a self-taught creative who thinks and operates far outside the influence of traditional education, realized that the first requirement for regenerating the ecosystem was an inversion of the temperature difference between the soil and rain. As long as the soil was exposed to the sun, the rain would never penetrate the thin layer of earth, and all organic matter would be washed away, further eroding the soil. If, on the other hand, he could find a tree able to survive the heat and create shade, then new life could emerge. After carefully studying the local environment and ecosystems in the tropical belt of Latin America, Lugari chose to plant Caribbean pine trees he had found in Nicaraguan forests. He planted the first seeds in Las Gaviotas, but despite all his attention and care, none survived the four months of heat and drought. He went back to Nicaragua, and when he studied the trees more closely, he discovered that the most flourishing pine trees had mushrooms growing at their roots. Lugari decided to mix his seeds with a "mushroom soup"; it worked. The planting of the trees started in 1987, and today, after 30 years and some eight

Plan A

million trees on 8,000 hectares (20,000 acres), Las Gaviotas sits amidst a reborn rainforest surrounded by barren savannas. This replanting program resulted in one of the most profitable investments ever in forest regeneration, while the benefits for the community are beyond expectations.

At the start of the project, 47 species inhabited the lands, including 11 non-native grasses. Now, researchers have counted more than 250 reborn, native plant species per hectare, more than in many parts of the Amazon, and this number continues to rise. All non-native species are gone. The regeneration of the ecosystem have strengthened the endemic species and crowded out the invasive ones, and nature has rediscovered its true evolutionary path. The small pockets of biodiversity left along the rivers has provided the biotas transported by the wind, birds, and bees. In addition, as the pine trees grew and began to protect the soil from the tropical sun, dormant seeds that had been buried for centuries came back to life, recreating an ecosystem with many other trees, flowers, shrubs, and animals. The villagers have rediscovered all kinds of perfectly edible, "new" fruits and plants in the forest that grow perfectly and without effort. They discovered a kind of potato bush, bearing a fruit tasting like chocolate; they found a spinach plant that doesn't look like the spinach we know, but has the same taste and nutrition; they also came upon a coffee plant that doesn't look like coffee. One might ask why the locals do not plant "real" potatoes from other places in South America; "real" spinach, originally from Persia; or "real" coffee beans from Africa. The response is simple: these are gifts from the forests which are perfectly adapted to the climatological conditions of the region and able to grow effortlessly without the need for any chemistry or genetics. The families at Las Gaviotas are not newborn hunter-gatherers. Rather, they are observing how the laws of physics drive nature, and they are reaping the fruits of their discovery. This is an investment opportunity in which the risk is low, and the performance is secure.

The Las Gaviotas experience shows that trees are not just allies when it comes to reversing global warming because they take carbon dioxide out of the air. Trees start the inversion of the temperature necessary to create the conditions for the soil to be restored and replenished with carbon. With that, dozens and dozens of species can spontaneously come back to life, creating an ongoing positive feedback loop and a self-regenerating healthy ecosystem. One of the main transformations of the forest is that the canopies and the roots of these new trees and plants—especially the undergrowth trapping the moisture—also replenishes the water table. The forest cover has allowed the laws of physics to bring back temperature differentials that generate more rain, as has been documented in over four decades of meteorological data, captured on site. A region once known for its bad water is now, according to Japanese water expert, Masaru Emoto, the source of water classified as the simplest and the most ecological with a healthy mineral balance. Emoto photographed a beautiful water crystal, symbolizing the fundamentals. The shape of the crystal—perfectly hexagonal in geometry—demonstrates to the experts who believe that the geometry of its frozen state can measure water quality, that this water is pure. Las Gaviotas distributes this healthy water for free to the local population, and gastrointestinal illnesses have disappeared as a result. To finance the distribution of subsidized free water to the local population, Las Gaviotas sells ten percent of it to the Wok restaurant chain in Bogota.

Las Gaviotas is using the laws of physics in another productive way. The trees that first provided the cover allowing the rainforest to come back now offer another valuable asset: the villagers tap resin from the pine trees, which is used to produce chemicals and biodiesel. Most biodiesel in the world is created through a chemical reaction of plant oil and methanol. The methanol splits the plant oil into glycerin and diesel, changing the esters so the oil will burn easily and power a combustion engine. In other words, nature is chemically changed to suit the demands of an engine. Methanol is expensive, and the necessary chemical reaction must be controlled and carefully monitored, requiring substantial capital investment.

Las Gaviotas doesn't use chemistry to produce biodiesel, but it does use physics, avoiding risky reactions and cutting high capital investments to less than ten percent of the market standard. It also has proven that small local supply units responding to local demand are competitive, ensuring money keeps circulating in the local economy, in stark contrast with the model of imported fuels, based on large facilities searching for ever higher economies of scale.

In a small, on-site facility, resin is collected from the pine trees through steam distillation and separated into solid colophon—an ingredient used in the paint industry, and turpentine—a highly flammable chemical, traditionally used to cleanse paint brushes. The purification is done by decanting, filtration, micro-filtration, temperature, and pressure, which leads to physical separation through specific weight and density in a matter of hours. The colophon dries and cools off in cardboard and is sold as an additive in the paint and paper industry. The turpentine is an extraordinary fuel that is already a naturally produced transester! This means there is no need for methanol or a chemical reaction to create higher quality biofuel at much lower costs. The fuel will power any gasoline or diesel engine.

This is not new. Mr. Soichiro Honda—the creator of the Honda Automobile Company after World War II—delivered motorcycles that ran on turpentine. Thanks to the pine forest covering 70 percent of Japan, there were grand reserves of this fuel. Las Gaviotas is self-sufficient in energy, with a fuel that can be simply and cheaply produced using the laws of nature. The village even goes to the next level of fuel production, with the blending of two, non-toxic substances. The biofuel is converted into biodiesel, mixing the turpentine with pine oil from the same trees and used vegetable cooking oils from restaurants in Bogota, which are brought back by trucks delivering Las Gaviotas water to the capital. This blend is ideal for diesel engines.

One could argue that Las Gaviotas is lucky to have tropical pine trees producing the turpentine. Other places where fuels like diesel and ethanol are made from corn or sugar cane are not as lucky, because they don't have pine trees. One might say this is exactly why we need to shift the traditional business model for land use with an economic model based on an integrated strategy for fuel, food, and jobs—it's inefficient to cultivate monoculture fields of corn and sugar cane which extract nutrients from the soil, depleting the carbon that has accumulated over decades and sometimes, centuries.

The case of Las Gaviotas shows that the regeneration of the world's forests—the restoration of the planet's natural skin—is more than the planting of trees to capture carbon emissions to protect the ecosystem. It is about the design of a business model where efficiency and competitiveness is determined by the ease of producing multiple outputs and benefits, which, when combined, can be offered at a low cost, since so much more value is generated. It may be surprising for many to note that it is easy to avoid the petrochemical cracking and fracking of petroleum and the chemical conversion of vegetable oils with simple, cheap, local production.

We should plant pine trees around the crops where the climate and soil suits this approach so that turpentine can be harvested and blended with oils from fruits, flowers, and plant seeds into biodiesel. In so doing, farmers are easily able to add additional cash flow to their operations. Imagine what this implies for local, territorial development when there is no longer the need to import any fuel. It is one of the greatest catalysts in the local economy. When Lyonpo Dr. Pema Gyamtsho, Minister of Bhutan's agriculture and forestry (a country that is 70 percent covered in pine forests), visited Las Gaviotas and realized the breakthrough that had been achieved there, he quickly concluded that the future of his Himalayan Kingdom does not lie in the importation of more oil from the Middle East, but rather in the harvesting of the fuel the country already possesses.

Argentina has her own opportunity to replicate the Las Gaviotas story in an investment proposal offering extraordinary returns. In the region of the Province of Formosa in the northeast of the country close to the border with Paraguay, a large territory of 60,000 hectares has been offered by private investors. The climatological, geographical, and soil conditions of this region resemble the barren savannas around Las Gaviotas, as was confirmed after a visit by Prof. Carlos Bernal, director of ZERI Latin America. Prof. Bernal—who has 20 years of experience of working in Las Gaviotas—has advised that, after the first analysis in Formosa, a rainforest can be similarly recreated through the planting of pine trees.

The ownership and local cultural environment carry great similarities, too. The region was like Las Gaviotas at the outset of the initiative: sparsely populated, with only 69 families in three small villages, each of them benefiting from a small school and health post. Water and communications were scarce and the population survived by hunting, gathering, and small-scale agriculture. The Bellsolá Ferrer family has owned the *Asociacion de Parques'* 60,000 hectares for years. The neighbors include the Wichi Native Community, owning a 5,000-hectare reserve.

For years, the Bellsolá family has attempted to regenerate the forest cover. They made an inventory of plant biodiversity and offered to manage regeneration of the forest in cooperation with national authorities, and researched local conditions in cooperation with the National University in Formosa. However, the challenge was that the local tree species—including Palo Santo, *Algarrobo* (carob), and mora (mulberries)—are very valuable and harvested beyond their carrying capacity, which only serves to fuel ongoing deforestation.

The Bellsolá family has collected seeds, created small tree nurseries, and organized internal distribution of seeds. An area of 1,500 hectares was planted to demonstrate it is possible to overcome climatological conditions which include harsh, hot and dry spells of up to nine months, and three months of torrential rains—again, similar to Las Gaviotas. The only difference is that this region can also experience a few weeks of frost each year. This determines the tree varieties chosen to kickstart the reforestation initiative. The Ministry of Environment and Sustainable Development of Argentina is committed to establishing tree nurseries in the country to speed up reforestation programs. This complementary effort will facilitate necessary investment.

An initial pollen study will offer an overview of plants that have been flourishing in this ecosystem over the centuries. The outcome of this study will provide the basis for a strategic development plan, including economic opportunities related to the chosen species. Also like in Las Gaviotas, it will be clear from the start that the species will return once the soil has been covered and protected. It is already known that highly-prized tree species like carob and Palo Santo grow in the wild in this region, providing multiple cash flows, supporting the investment logic.

The program needs to include a policy permitting people to return to their land. The 69 families are not in any position to undertake large-scale regeneration of the native forest. This is why the first focus should be—and the owners are in agreement with this—to ensure that the local community, as well as the local school, have their own basic water and food guaranteed, creating confidence. Subsequently, the local population senses the opportunity to full employment in the reforestation initiative before newcomers may arrive to participate in this project to transform a regional environment and economy.

While the carob and Palo Santo are obvious starts, there is also the option to identify—on the basis of the pollen study—which trees and shrubs were a part of this ecosystem over the past centuries. Tropical pines that resist spells of cold weather could, within three to four years, see the first harvest of turpentine or biodiesel. The local community— which currently has no access to power other than through generators running on fossil fuels—will provide the first customers. Again, inspired by Las Gaviotas, a second revenue stream will gradually emerge as the growing forest begins to produce drinking water. Today, most drinking water in Formosa comes from imported plastic bottles which drain the region of financial resources. The key to re-launching a local economy characterized by poverty and unemployment is to ensure the very basic services are provided locally, starting with water, food, and health. From these initial steps, a portfolio of competitive industries will emerge, providing food, energy, and drinking water while replenishing the topsoil, sequestering CO_2, and regenerating biodiversity. This is Las Gaviotas' scientifically proven and economically viable strategy.

As is the case in the Las Gaviotas' inspiring example, physics and chemistry can work together to ensure a sustainable and competitive outcome in Formosa. The critical message of this initiative is that the understanding and application of physics comes first. If we continue to rely only upon chemistry and genetics to produce food and fuel without considering opportunities offered by physics, the destruction of the planet will continue while we spend too much money and energy on temporary solutions that will not transform society. The production completely changes when trees are planted, and the laws of physics are brought back into the equation. It is only then that nature's genius will lead to environmental restoration and regeneration and productivity that will let communities flourish.

The power of nature makes this a superb investment with ongoing value. In Las Gaviotas, a core investment of 1,100 dollars per hectare of tree planting set a regeneration of biodiversity into motion, which is, today, as diverse as the Amazon rainforest. The estimated investment for Formosa is similar. There is also an additional key element in the valuation and risk-analysis of such an investment.

Land that has no water and no electricity provides no chance for a livelihood and has hardly any value. The value of land providing water, power, and generating full employment, building social capital in an environment of peace and tranquility, will only increase. A range of commercial products and activities emerges: the resin of the trees, the production of drinking water, the harvesting of food, the generation of turpentine and vegetable oil blended into a biodiesel of the simplest type and the lowest cost. When JP Morgan studied the Las Gaviotas case, a team of experts concluded the value of the land had increased 3,000 times since the acquisition. This figure was based solely on cash flow generated and did not include any social or environmental benefits. The analysis demonstrated a break-even accumulated cash flow after only 11 years (all investments are earned in cash) with an unlimited flux of cash generated after that. There are no stock exchanges offering similar investment opportunities!

This program transforms land without value into a regenerated ecosystem providing food, wood, water, and fuel, rebuilding the local economy, improving health, and generating jobs. This is an investment in transformation; this is the realm of investors we have named the Captains of Legacy. The land is available, science has confirmed the concept, a major part of the homework has been done, and the support of the government is solid. Formosa can be the starting point of an environmental renaissance in Argentina!

Plan A

Clustering regeneration of forests with food and fuel

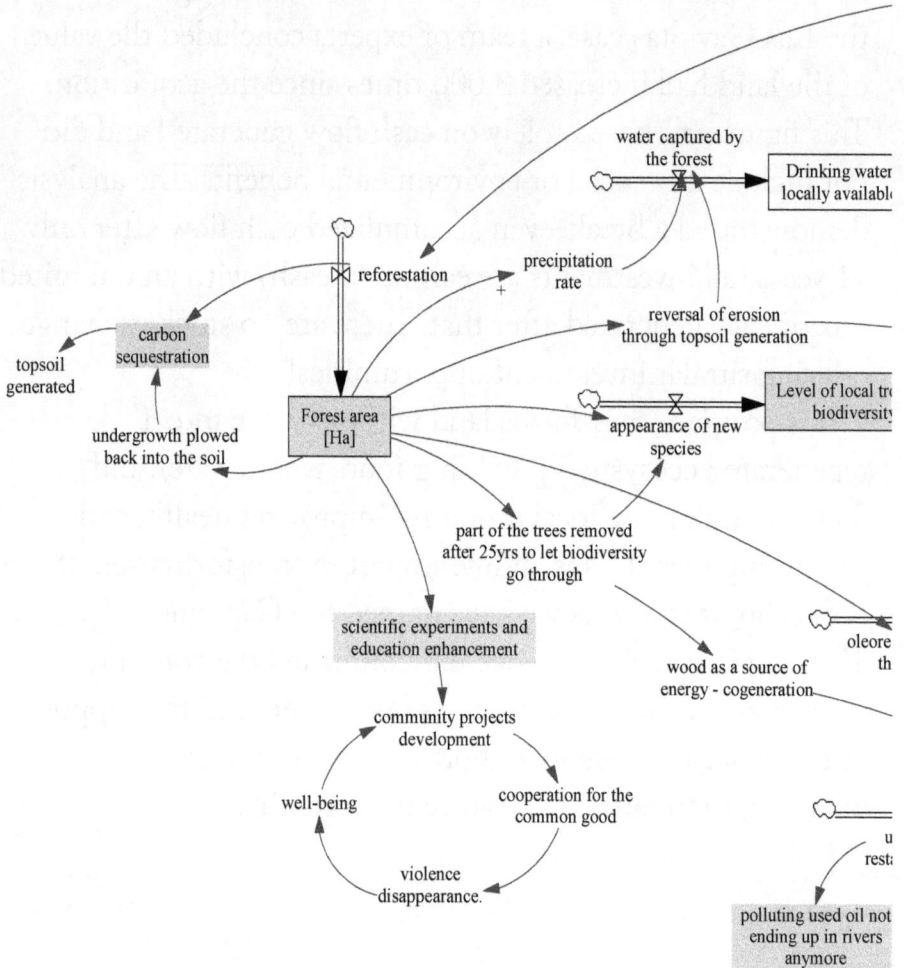

water captured by
the forest

Drinking wate
locally available

reforestation

precipitation
rate

reversal of erosion
through topsoil generation

+

carbon
sequestration

topsoil
generated

Level of local tr
biodiversity

Forest area
[Ha]

appearance of new
species

undergrowth plowed
back into the soil

part of the trees removed
after 25yrs to let biodiversity
go through

scientific experiments and
education enhancement

oleore
th

community projects
development

wood as a source of
energy - cogeneration

well-being

cooperation for the
common good

violence
disappearance.

u
rest;

polluting used oil not
ending up in rivers
anymore

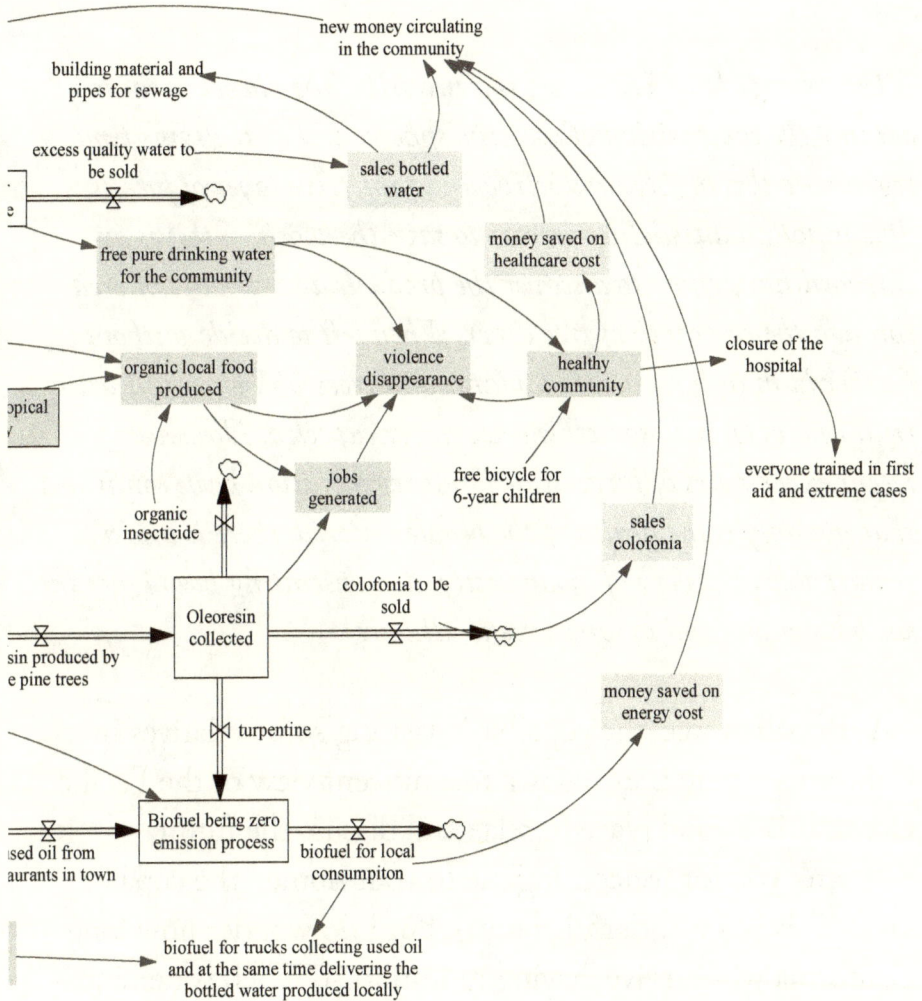

new money circulating
in the community

building material and
pipes for sewage

excess quality water to
be sold

sales bottled
water

free pure drinking water
for the community

money saved on
healthcare cost

organic local food
produced

violence
disappearance

healthy
community

closure of the
hospital

opical

jobs
generated

free bicycle for
6-year children

sales
colofonia

everyone trained in first
aid and extreme cases

organic
insecticide

Oleoresin
collected

colofonia to be
sold

sin produced by
e pine trees

money saved on
energy cost

turpentine

Biofuel being zero
emission process

sed oil from
aurants in town

biofuel for local
consumpiton

biofuel for trucks collecting used oil
and at the same time delivering the
bottled water produced locally

Fable 10
Oil growing on trees

The cover of land with trees is a necessity. The planet needs to balance the composition of the atmosphere, and at the same time, regenerate this highly productive and protective layer of forests. This is not an altruistic program to save the world—this is an extraordinary effort to discover the products and services offered through the regrowth of tree cover. When left to decide without further human intervention, plants and trees will emerge bearing fruit and even fuel, something we never expected. However, recent experiences of large-scale forest regeneration have confirmed that not only is the health of the people restored, there is also a remarkable discovery of biodiversity, demonstrating how ignorant we have been (and to some extent, still are).

A Brazilian tree, the copaiba, is visiting some relatives in California where they enjoy a magnificent view of the Pacific Coast. It is a good place to relax and discuss the future.

"Thank you for welcoming me to your home," the copaiba says. "This is a wonderful country, but I do wonder how long California will survive, having to import so much water and fuel."

"We earn so much money here, in the United States, we could be considered one of the richest countries in the world! We can buy water and fuel from those who have it, and have people ship it to us," responds the eupho tree.

"Well, you may be rich, but will there always be enough water and fuel in the world to satisfy your big and ever-growing appetite?"

"If there is no longer enough, we will just plant more shrubs and trees," responds the eupho. "And we will have all of the fuel we need."

"Why would you wait until it is too late? You and I both know that when a tree is planted, it takes years before you can harvest it."

"You are right on all counts, you know. People consume too much fuel and pump too much water over long distances. And it is true: they do tend to act only when it is too late."

"The people living in the Amazon have been tapping me for ages," the copaiba says. "They drill a little hole in my stem and the fresh diesel fuel that flows out can be put straight into an engine."

"You mean instead of going to the gas station they stop by the tree and fill up? That's just a fantasy, though it is an interesting one! Hollywood would immediately make a movie about that," laughs the eupho.

"You can laugh all you like, but they had better first design cars that are fuel efficient instead of these guzzlers they drive around here. We can only offer twenty liters per tap, and then only maybe twice a year."

"Well, I am richer in fuel than you are," the eupho boasts.

"And I do not need to be in any lush rainforest in the Amazon to grow. I am able to grow on dry land, right here, in California."

"Whenever one can have a local solution using a local plant, especially a friendly one like you, by all means, go for it! There is no need to look overseas."

"I have heard this question asked so often! What do you imagine those people, who make a lot of money from fuel now, think about this?"

"But surely all those rich people who make a fortune selling petroleum cannot stop a fuel like yours, one that uses the best nature has to offer without harming the Earth. Do they really not care about rising sea levels and climate change?" the copaiba wants to know.

"Well, it seems they don't. They're just not willing to trade their Texan oil wells for Californian or Brazilian plants."

"It may be that the older generation doesn't care, but I'm sure their children and grandchildren do."

... And it has only just begun!

Chapter 10
The next generation of the Internet

The Internet is a critical component of modernization. The online economy drives modern societies. And while this unbridled growth has been ongoing for 25 years, it does not seem like there is any sign of its slowing down. The 24/7 communication driven by the Internet is one of the economy's steadfast growth factors. It is no surprise that the energy consumption of online communication has risen from one to two percent of global energy consumption, and it may even reach six percent by 2030; there always seems to be a downside to an upside.

This fast-track roll-out of connectivity is a challenge for countries like Argentina with an outdated infrastructure that does not reach all the corners of the country and does not provide the necessary connectivity. Argentina deals with a large rate of youth unemployment. Young people are eager to embrace the world of hackers and gamers and 3D designers and passionate firmware writers, but the brightest and most talented entrepreneurs leave the country to set up businesses in North America, as their home country lacks the infrastructure and resources to develop their innovative initiatives.

Plan A

This is the case with Tomi Pierucci, Diego Saez-Gil, and Alejo Vermin, who created BlueSmart. They raised all of their funds in the United States but kept a foot on the ground in Buenos Aires. It is a negative trend that could leave Argentina falling further behind.

A better digital communications infrastructure is the answer. The new 5G cellphone network—in development for over a decade—promises broader bandwidths and faster speeds by 2020. However, updating the Argentine networks to this new standard will require billions of dollars that the country doesn't have. Private investors are stepping in, but this will only lead to higher rates that a large majority of the population cannot afford. Strangely enough, 5G may not even be enough for countries with the financial capacity to upgrade their mobile networks. It is estimated that a person in the industrialized world will own an average of seven connected devices by 2025: a computer, a cell phone, a camera, a fridge, a car, keys, heating and cooling systems, security devices, gate and door controls, etc. Using artificial intelligence (AI), all of these devices will talk to each other in "the Internet of things." In your car, you will find a message that there is no more milk in your fridge. On your phone, you can turn the heat on in your apartment before you come home. The coffee will start brewing according to your roasting preferences while you are in the shower. And we are not even talking about millions of self-driving cars finding their way through constant communication over mobile networks. All of this communication requires bandwidth, and there are not enough frequencies below 10GHz—the spectrum used for all civil communication—

to enable all of this mobile traffic. The 5G network, which promises a speed of one gigabit of data transmission per second, seems already saturated before it has even officially launched.

These contradictory trends of failing to reach the poor as well as failing to meet the expectations of the well-to-do create a unique opportunity. We need additional frequencies. We also need to reduce the energy consumption of connectivity. Few people realize that each WiFi router consumes the equivalent of three, good-old, 60-watt lamps, kept on 24 hours a day. Offices and even homes have an increasing number of routers. This is why, when it comes to electricity consumption, the Internet is the fastest growing sector. Something bold is required to reverse this. The good news is that there is a solution that will meet both the need for added communication frequency capacity and the need to reduce energy consumption. The technology that has been invented in France in 2005 will provide Argentina with the opportunity to bypass investments in 3G, 4G, and even 5G mobile networks, and leapfrog to a future of fast and wide connectivity. It will empower the Argentinian minister of modernization to quickly embrace a breakthrough that is cheap since it can be funded with the energy savings.

Almost two hundred years ago, Samuel Morse demonstrated it was possible to communicate over vast distances with light signals. By turning lights slowly on and off, messages could be communicated through "Morse code" to a distant observer. If we multiply the speed of this blinking to 100 million times per second (100 MHz), enormous amounts of information can be transmitted at the speed of light, invisible to the human eye. This is the invention of LiFi.

LiFi comes with many benefits. First of all, the introduction of LiFi will reduce energy consumption by around 80 percent. LiFi communication happens through LED lights, providing an immediate saving of power of 50 percent. A total savings of 80 percent can be achieved through intelligent energy management. When you leave a building, you turn the light off and immediately shut down energy consumption for lumens and data, as the distribution of electricity and information is now operated through the same network. Incidentally, this will make hacking just about impossible. Data is transmitted through existing electricity cables, using current ADSL technology. The high-speed, LiFi experience will happen when the data is transmitted through LED lights at the end of the cables. The same logic also applies in reverse—an optical fiber cable can be used to supply power, limiting it all to just one cable...whatever is available.

Governments worldwide provide public light in towns and cities along streets and roads. Light creates a sense of safety and helps to control criminal behavior. The cost of public light is never an issue. Governments needing to cut expenses don't turn the lights off in cities. This means that Argentina can introduce LiFi as a public connectivity service out of existing budgets without the need for additional investments. The breakthrough of LiFi is that it integrates high-speed Internet into the public light system. In other words, there's an infrastructure that has already been paid for, and there's a budget!

The energy savings will make it possible to finance the conversion to LED and LiFi out of the existing cash flow, with a payback time between three and five years. After that period, a better-combined electricity and data service can be offered, ongoing, at 20 percent of today's costs. This is a game-changer for any country in which the people are hungry for connectivity. Instead of facing the almost impossible challenge of upgrading an outdated infrastructure with billions of unavailable dollars, the country can now quickly and cheaply modernize its connectivity structure which is critical for supporting much-needed economic development.

The advantage of LiFi further increases when the old copper power cables are gradually replaced with glass fiber cables able to carry 12-volts of direct current and data. A glass fiber network will allow for Internet communication at the speed of light—at least 200 times faster than the radio waves we use today, but the critical point is that Argentina can hugely improve the speed and capacity of the existing Internet infrastructure without the need for massive investments.

The introduction of LiFi means that every lamppost in the street with an LED bulb—the LED lights in public transit and public buildings—becomes an Internet transmission point. Even better, every light will turn into a satellite! There will be connectivity everywhere, there will be speed, and there will be services the present system cannot provide with the same accuracy. This connectivity will be highly precise. When three satellites, 20 to 40 kilometers in space locate a car, it is normal there would be a margin of error when measuring of a meter to as much as ten meters.

Plan A

If, on the other hand, a smartphone and two street lights are only six to eight meters away, then the precision of determining the exact location of a moving (or still) object is unparalleled. Through the connection of the LED light, your device will know exactly where it is to the centimeter. This is a different experience when compared to the map app driven by GPS technology on your current mobile phone with a blue dot that dances nicely in the vicinity of where you are and disappears when you travel on the metro. A whole portfolio of geolocation services will open up, valued at tens of billions of dollars.

This precision allows governments to offer valuable services. For instance, the visually impaired can be precisely guided through the streets. The same applies to visiting tourists who are navigating the cities, much like "blind" people. There are plenty of commercial applications, as well. With LiFi, it will be easy to find the Tabasco in the supermarket. You may be walking along the street when your phone will alert you when passing your favorite shoe store that is offering a sale. Searching for a parking place will be a thing of the past. When you enter the parking garage, LiFi will guide you to your spot, and you will never again search in vain for your car on the wrong floor of the garage. Yes, this could become annoying, as well, but there will always be an "off" switch. The important point is that LiFi will offer a new platform to allow for localized services.

LiFi will change business as well. Today, all goods in warehouses need to be scanned to be located, and cashiers scan the products you buy in the supermarket. In the near future, a little diode will be added to all products, which means that all products will be able to communicate with the LED lights, eliminating the need to scan. You always know where everything is, and the tiny battery will power the tiny "here I am" call for at least ten years.

When a new platform emerges, there is the opportunity to change the rules of the game, and it is time the rules are changed when it comes to data collection and the related financial benefit. Today, almost all "big data" is controlled by a handful of American Internet giants: Google, Apple, Microsoft, Facebook, etc. In return for an email address and/ or in return for the service to browse the Internet freely, we give all of our personal data away to these companies for free, giving them increasingly more control over our lives and the ability to make a lot of money, because they can sell precise information about our behaviors. You would be surprised— and most certainly protest—if someone had the ability to use your liver or another part of your body for free and without your permission, but you do not own a large part of your mind. You do not fully own the (financial) power of the choices you make. This is an unhealthy situation that LiFi could change.

LiFi will bring the data to you, so you will not need to search anymore. Does this mean you will not need Google anymore? You will make your shopping list on your phone, and whenever you are close to a store that has something on your list, LiFi will tell you that you need to visit the store. The same applies to governments and the public domain—when a tourist arrives in Buenos Aires, he knows nothing and uses his phone to find out where his hotel and everything else is.

Guess who makes money on these searches? Google! Not the city of Buenos Aires that provides the information for free. Google doesn't know where the tourist's hotel is. Google doesn't know the public transit system. Google doesn't have all of this information. The genius of the search giant is its ability to bring all of this information together in a search engine-operated platform controlled by...Google.

The introduction of LiFi makes it possible to bring information back under the control of those who source it. We will recover the votes we have lost. When a local government invests in new lighting systems, it can control the distribution of local data through local LiFi networks. This will allow local communities to own their information, exchange it with those who share the benefits, and deliver data and information precisely to those who should receive it, to cut down on spam. Even better, the value of the streetlights—which was calculated as a cost to the community—will now turn into a valuable asset.

An additional advantage of LiFi is that it will provide much better security from external hacking. Unlike radio waves, light waves—LiFi signals—do not travel through walls. This means a signal is contained in the room or at the location. Out of the reach of the light beam, there is no personal connection.

Light waves are less invasive, which leads to another important benefit of LiFi: reducing the concern about the impact of electromagnetic fields caused by mobile phone radio wave networks, particularly on children. For example, the European Commission recently issued a strong recommendation to limit the exposure to a maximum of

0.62 volts per square meter. The French parliament has set that level as a legal standard. California is imposing strict limitations on the use of radio waves.

However, research shows that exposure can be much higher in many places. Radio waves can disrupt cell-to-cell communication in our bodies, which can cause disease. Again, LiFi waves do not interfere with bodily frequencies. Some have gone as far as to claim that the debate around the health impact of radio waves is comparable to the discussions around smoking in the 70s. The industry knows it causes damage, but it also recognizes that any limitation will hinder their profitable business margins, so they lobby and resist.

Light waves also don't interfere with equipment. A common problem in hospitals is that an excess of competing radio waves could disturb the functioning of critical medical equipment. A brief disturbance in an electrical system can change a critical dose of medicine fed through an automated drip. This needs to be avoided at all costs.

LiFi offers a perfect and healthy solution for communication and connectivity within hospitals. To set up a LiFi network in an average hospital costs about 300,000 dollars, an investment that can be paid back in three to five years out of the energy savings. There are additional efficiency savings and new services, as it will be easy for hospital staff to locate equipment, medicines, and the like. Today, nurses lose substantial time going from room-to-room, searching for the equipment and/ or medicines they need.

People who are first introduced to LiFi tend to think it is the next version of the Wifi with which they are familiar, an interpretation inspired by the similarity of the names, but LiFi is not a replacement for WiFi. Instead, LiFi offers a completely new platform for connectivity with different services and different players.

Argentina could embark on an initial, rapid modernization plan to launch LiFi in a few cities and a few rural communities where there is no connectivity at all, as a starting point for a nationwide rollout. LiFi offers the country the unique opportunity to join the core of the global Internet economy, driving innovation and economic growth. The country can make this jump without the need for billions of dollars of investments to upgrade the existing infrastructure. It can simply turn an available asset with a low value—the existing, public light network—into a new platform for the delivery of numerous valuable services.

Argentina can do more with what it already has. It can create more connectivity, which means more economic development and more income for its citizens and communities. Metro stations, hospitals, and schools can be quickly converted, and hundreds of schools that had no power and no connectivity could now leapfrog, bringing modernity to the Internet of everyone! And the bill for this will be paid by the energy savings. This is the kind of budgetary intervention that governments with tight budgets enjoy. This is the kind of investment in which any investor would like to participate.

The Transformation of Argentina's Economy

Plan A

Clustering energy savings with hi-speed Internet

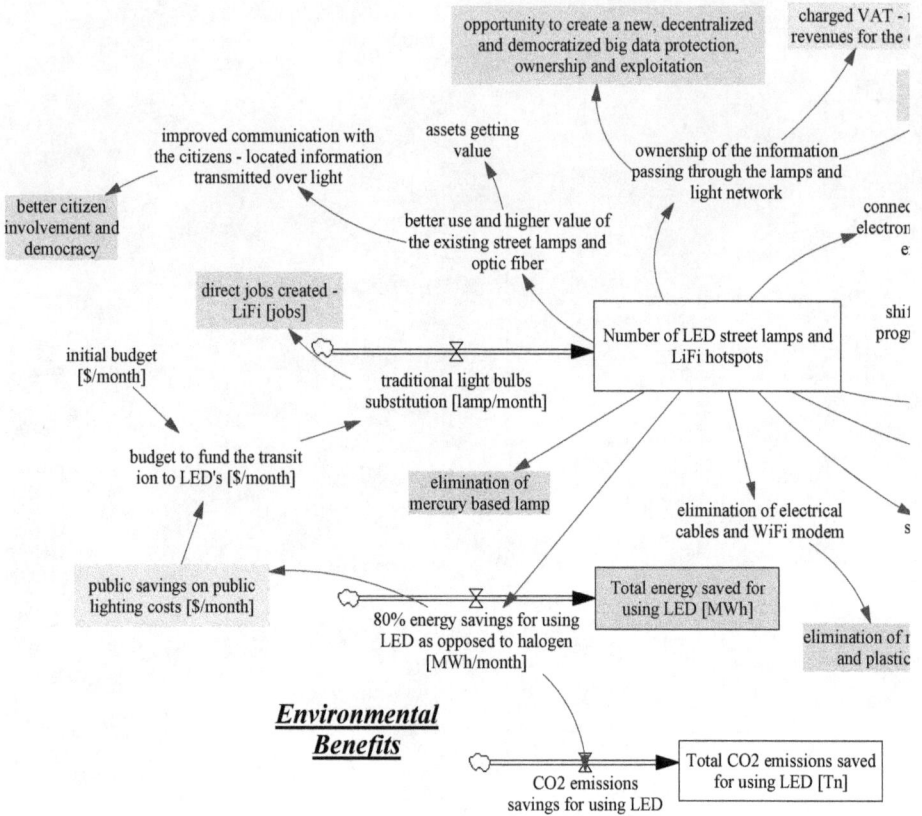

opportunity to create a new, decentralized
and democratized big data protection,
ownership and exploitation

charged VAT - 1
revenues for the

improved communication with
the citizens - located information
transmitted over light

assets getting
value

ownership of the information
passing through the lamps and
light network

connec
electron
e

better citizen
involvement and
democracy

better use and higher value of
the existing street lamps and
optic fiber

shi
prog

direct jobs created -
LiFi [jobs]

Number of LED street lamps and
LiFi hotspots

initial budget
[$/month]

traditional light bulbs
substitution [lamp/month]

budget to fund the transit
ion to LED's [$/month]

elimination of
mercury based lamp

elimination of electrical
cables and WiFi modem

s

public savings on public
lighting costs [$/month]

Total energy saved for
using LED [MWh]

80% energy savings for using
LED as opposed to halogen
[MWh/month]

elimination of r
and plastic

Environmental Benefits

CO2 emissions
savings for using LED

Total CO2 emissions saved
for using LED [Tn]

new
cities

data security in
 private areas

Public services to citizens

health disturbances
decrease

new local skills and professions in
TIC industry

ctivity without
nagnetic waves
missions

connectivity in mines,
hospitals and nurseries

indirect jobs LiFi
[jobs]

<public savings on public
lighting costs [$/month]>

ft to 3D
ramming

solution for the
congested radio waves

impulse for the IoT
emergence

innovative entrepreneurship
platform

new money ciruclating in
the local economy - LiFi

100x better
transmission speed

Multiplier effect on the local economy

geolocation
services

smart lighting
services

emergence of innovative
social and industrial
applications

guidance for visually impaired
persons in public transport

4% sales increase

netals
s

logistic and
authentification

guidance in
supermarket

deliver what the
consumer wants to buy

Fable 11

At the speed of light

In school, we all learn that the fastest, measurable speed is that of light, and yet we do not use it. We have all learned the coded message of SOS translated into Morse, and yet we do not use it anymore. The opportunity to complement the present radio communications infrastructure through WiFi, 3G, 4G, Bluetooth, hotspots and the like is an opportunity to do more than offering yet another way to connect. It is a means to save energy (and fund the investment), it reduces health risks and protects data, putting the responsibility back into the hands of the people who provided the data in the first place.

The owl is sitting on his branch, high up in the tree and notices that everyone is watching their personal screens. He spots one rat that is looking at the sky.

"Don't you have one of these things that connects you to the world?" remarks the owl.

"I don't know why everyone is so keen on getting to the Internet."

"The Internet—you mean the network that connects everyone to everything, puts you in touch with wisdom and experiences from around the world?"

"I think that people who only look at what is out there on the other side through these little screens forget to look at what is here next to us."

"People are so connected, and they can learn so much about each other. It makes the world much smaller."

"Connected? I think it makes the world dumb."

"That's not true, and it's certainly not very nice to say."

"Well, I see families over breakfast, couples in restaurants, kids in the car, and everyone is glued to their screens. We don't discover what we have anymore. We have even have forgotten how to look people in the eyes and smile."

"I know—a wonderful and honest smile is contagious. However, thanks to the Internet you can instantly figure out what the weather will be, or where you can buy a book—that's progress."

"Progress? Is it really better when you can order a book, have it delivered to your home, and get a like on your page? I would much prefer a visit to the local bookstore and a tap on my shoulder from those who really care."

"You will not be able to stop this Internet. Everything that we have will be connected through the cloud!"

"And how will these things communicate?"

"It all works like a radio: sound and radio waves."

"If I ever want to communicate, then I want to do it at the speed of light."

"Light is the fastest, but it has no Internet."

"Have you ever wondered why we use radio waves that jam the air, confuse the birds, and give us headaches?"

"Soon, we will have self-driving cars, we'll be able to see if our children are happy and safe, asleep at home while we're out in the forest."

"Why do you want to drive a car by connecting cameras to

satellites when you have streetlights and headlamps?"

"Because smart people put satellites in orbit and have cameras that can look all around you!"

"Look, I'm tired of people celebrating expensive technologies for the rich. I want safe streets with lights and cars that talk to each other to be safe on the road. And most important, I want to enjoy breakfast with the family again."

... And it only has just begun!

Epilogue

This book is but a 50,000-word summary of the full reports, overloaded with details constituting the bulk of information submitted to the government. Each chapter of perhaps 10 to 20 pages in this book has a tenfold of analysis and data to support it.

The ten sectors and four fields of action are only a first review. More initiatives have been identified and will be identified, but everything starts with a first set. This one will offer direction, and once a few concrete results have been obtained, others will quickly emerge.

However, we all know the dilemma of a bulky and loaded set of reports…it takes time to read. Therefore, those who are keen to learn more about each of the projects, from the pre-feasibility study and profit and loss statement made for stone paper to wanting to establish contact with the core members of Argentinian mushroom farming, and would like to visit one of the project sites, feel free to contact Luis Castelli at the the Argentinian Ministry of Environment and Sustainable Development: luisc@ambiente.gob.ar.

We believe the next steps of this endeavor are to ensure that the investors follow and the government creates the framework to facilitate action. There is a huge task before us: share the insights and improve the proposals, but in the meantime, let us make certain that the perfect does not stand in the way of the good—initiatives must unfold, and decisions to proceed must be taken.

The ZERI Network is prepared to support this process in any way it can, knowing that success will be measured (internally) by its obsolescence: the sooner the core team members are no longer needed, the better the job we have performed, since this implies that local experts and entrepreneurs will have taken over the leadership.

The Transformation of Argentina's Economy

The strongest tree

How can I ever be the strongest tree in this forest?

The more leaves I have, the more energy I get from the sun.

The more leaves I have, the more leaves will fall to the ground.

Ants, earthworms, and mushrooms convert the leaves into new food for me.

The more food I have, the more fruit I can grow.

The more fruit, the more the birds will visit me.

The more birds, the more droppings, and the more droppings, the more bacteria in the soil.

The more bacteria in the soil, the more enriched the groundwater will be.

The more food in the water, the more the flowers will grow, and the more flowers, the more bees.

The more bees, the more pollination, and the more seeds.

With nature's further procreation, my family and I will be the strongest in the forest.

Everyone gives me many gifts, made from things I did not need or that would have been wasted.

All of these actions contribute to my being the strongest, even though some are small, some are ugly, and some I cannot tell the difference between head and tail.

If I were to chase the earthworms away because I do not like or understand them, I could not be the strongest tree in the forest.

If you give away what you do not need, you get a lot back and together we can be the best.

The strongest tree gives what is not needed and in return, receives benefits from others.

The tree realizes that everyone can help, from the smallest to the most beautiful and perhaps even the ugliest.

... And it only has just begun!

Plan A

226

Index

Plan A

Plan A

Plan A

Plan A

About the author and the editor

Gunter Pauli (1956) is an established author who published his first books in 1987. His latest sequel of three editions of *The Blue Economy* has been translated into 43 languages and has reached over a million readers. Pauli is an entrepreneur who embraces groundbreaking and pioneering initiatives. While *The Huffington Post* named him the Steve Jobs of sustainability, his Latin American friends often refer to him as the Che Guevara of sustainability. He is dedicated to the transformation of society, designs a fundamentally new business model, and goes out of his way to turn vision into reality. Pauli witnessed, learned from, pushed forward, and/or started up over 200 projects in every corner of the world. He identified 12 trends that explain why these initiatives have taken ground, expand, and speed up. Pauli surfs the waves, intuitively thriving on the transformative and unstoppable trends that no statistics or big data seem to identify. Pauli believes that the transformation of society only succeeds when we reach out and inspire children at an early age. He has written about 280 fables based on an agreement with the Chinese Government, which has committed to publish 365 by 2022. He is a father of six, married to Katherine Bach, and has resided in Japan since 1994.

Jurriaan Kamp (1959) left a successful career as a South Asian correspondent and chief economics editor at the leading Dutch newspaper, *NRC Handelsblad*, to found the "solutions journalism" magazine *Ode*, which was later re-named *The Intelligent Optimist*. Under his guidance, the magazine has more than once won the prestigious Maggie Award for journalism. In 2015, Kamp launched a daily online solutions news service, *The Optimist Daily*. Kamp has regularly come in ahead of the curve on stories that advance new visions of our world, including a "More and Better" approach to sustainability. He published *Because People Matter: Building an Economy that Works for Everyone; Small Change: How Fifty Dollars Changes the World;* and most recently *The Intelligent Optimist's Guide to Life: How to find health and success in a world that's a better place than you think.* Kamp studied international law at Leiden University in the Netherlands. He is a father of four and lives with his beloved, Nancy McGrath, in Santa Barbara, California.

www.ingramcontent.com/pod-product-compliance
Lightning Source LLC
Chambersburg PA
CBHW032130020426
42334CB00016B/1104